MW01036911

Abiding in CHRIST

Becoming Like Christ through an Abiding Relationship with Him

PAUL CHAPPELL

Copyright © 2006 by Striving Together Publications. All Scripture quotations are taken from the King James Version.

First published in 2006 by Striving Together Publications, a ministry of Lancaster Baptist Church, Lancaster, CA 93535. Striving Together Publications is committed to providing tried, trusted, and proven books that will further equip local churches to carry out the Great Commission. Your comments and suggestions are valued.

All rights reserved. No part of this book may be reproduced, stored in a retrieval system, or transmitted in any form or by any means—electronic, mechanical, photocopy, recording, or otherwise—without written permission of the publisher, except for brief quotations in printed reviews.

Striving Together Publications
4020 E. Lancaster Blvd.
Lancaster, CA 93535
800.201.7748

Cover design by Andrew Jones and Jeremy Lofgren
Layout by Craig Parker
Edited by Andrew Jones, Kayla Nelson,
Cary Schmidt, and Danielle Chappell
Special thanks to our proofreaders.

We recognize that many of the stories and illustrations mentioned in this book are derived from a myriad of sources and are not original with the author. To preserve the accuracy and authenticity of each illustration the facts remain unchanged. We do not take credit for those illustrations whose sources we cannot locate.

ISBN 1-59894-019-8

Printed in the United States of America

Table of Contents

To my grandfather, Paul B. Chappell,
a farmer and a preacher who taught me
the principles of the Vine and the branches.

INTRODUCTION

We live in a fast-paced society. We're used to quick results. It seems that much of our time and money is spent trying to save time—to do things faster, more efficient, and with less effort. We hurry through our daily tasks, so we can move on to something more important. Our "to-do" lists are longer than the amount of time we have to get them done, and there's seemingly no end in sight.

"Abide" is not part of our modern vocabulary. Few people abide anywhere with anyone in today's culture. Who has time to abide?

Friend, if you find yourself in the rat race of time, pressured by a life that seems at times to be spinning out of control, then you've opened the right book. You need to rediscover this wonderful word—abide. You have an open invitation to abide in a living, intimate relationship with Jesus Christ—your Creator and God.

Stop for a minute, and think about this question: *What if, for one day, Jesus was your shadow?* Like a silhouetted image on the wall—He followed your every move. How would you act? What would you say? Would you ask for His help as you started tasks? If you made a decision, would you seek His advice? If you came across someone you knew, would you introduce Him as your Saviour? If your current prayer life translated to conversation, how long would it last?

If the answers to these questions are difficult, pull up a chair and ask God to help you learn what it means to "abide in Christ." The disciples were common men, yet they learned how to abide with the Saviour.

So can you.

How?

Read these verses from John 15 slowly. Notice what Jesus is telling us…

> *I am the true vine, and my Father is the husbandman. Every branch in me that beareth not fruit he taketh away: and every branch that beareth fruit, he purgeth it, that it may bring forth more fruit. Now ye are clean through the word which I have spoken unto you. Abide in me, and I in you. As the branch cannot bear fruit of itself, except it abide in the vine; no more can ye, except ye abide in me. I am the vine, ye are the branches: He that abideth in me, and I in him, the same bringeth forth much fruit: for without me ye can do nothing. If a man abide not in me, he is cast forth as a branch, and is withered; and men gather them, and cast them into the fire, and they are burned. If ye abide in me, and my words abide in you, ye shall ask what ye will, and it shall be done unto you. Herein is my Father glorified, that ye bear much fruit; so shall ye be my disciples. As the Father hath loved me, so*

have I loved you: continue ye in my love. If ye keep my commandments, ye shall abide in my love; even as I have kept my Father's commandments, and abide in his love. These things have I spoken unto you, that my joy might remain in you, and that your joy might be full.—JOHN 15:1–11

The secret to abiding in Christ is found in these verses. Jesus wants to spend time with you more than you can imagine. Yes, TIME—your most valued commodity. He wants it—from you. He loves you, He died for you; the least you can do is abide with Him.

Read this book in a quiet place—a place where you can feel God's presence near and hear His heart beating for you. Don't be afraid to draw near. Let Christ walk you through these paragraphs. He wants more than just to affiliate with you; He wants to abide with you.

In these pages you will unravel the principles necessary for an abiding relationship with Christ. Determine to be connected with Jesus like never before. Give Him your time. Give Him your attention. Give Him your life. After all, He gave His life for you.

One Christian lady, referring to her own abiding relationship with Christ, made this statement: "Connected with Him in His love, I am more than conqueror; without Him, I am nothing. Like some railway tickets in America, I am *not good if detached.*"

PART ONE

Abiding in Christ

CHAPTER ONE

Abiding in His Presence

T here are thousands of words in the English language, yet I would guess that the word *abide* is probably not one you used last week. We have all used the phrases, "let's go" or "hurry up!" We tend to use vernacular that keeps us going, but words like *abide* usually escape us.

Webster defines the word *abide* this way: "to remain or settle down." Our world today places such emphasis on being upwardly mobile, that the very thought of remaining with something or someone has negative connotations. Americans are on the move—from relationship to relationship, state to state, company to company, spouse to spouse, and church to church. The tragedy is that fewer people are finding God and abiding in a close-knit relationship with Him.

Even television has trained us to the point that about six minutes from now, you will need a commercial break from this book! You will want to set these pages aside, go to the fridge, and get some milk and cookies. Culture conditions us to be in motion—constantly on the go.

The Lord Jesus Christ spoke the words in our text. No fewer than eight times in this passage He tells His disciples, "Abide in Me." "Remain with Me." "Settle down into a relationship with Me." "Let it be normal and natural that we would commune together day by day and moment by moment."

In this passage, Jesus was somewhere between the upper room and the Garden of Gethsemane, quite possibly surrounded by vineyards. In John 15, Jesus was not inviting His disciples to "try Him out" or to "see what it might be like." He was inviting them to remain with Him.

What does it mean to abide, personally, with Jesus Christ? Is it simply a figurative concept, or is it an experience we can truly enjoy? Let's discover what it means to abide in the presence of Christ.

The Supremacy of His Presence

In verse 1 Jesus said, "*I am the true vine….*" Notice the words, "*I am.*" Jesus Christ is not presenting Himself as merely another way or another religion. The words "*I am*" are very powerful words in the Bible. Earlier in the book of John, Jesus said, "*I am the bread of life.*" He declared, "*I am the light of the world.*" He also said, "*I am the door.*" And in John 14:6, Jesus proclaimed, "*…I am the way, the truth, and the life: no man cometh unto the Father, but by me.*" Jesus' statements are definitive. They are powerful and exclusive. His claims are supreme, and when you enter His presence, you are entering into the greatest presence in the universe!

He said, "*I am the true vine.*" The word *true* means "genuinely true." Jesus Christ is not a false vine or just another vine. Jesus is the genuine, true Vine. There are many self-proclaimed saviors and man-made religions in the world today, but Jesus is the truth.

If we, as branches, are going to gain sustenance and life, we must abide in the true Vine.

Some say it doesn't matter which vine you abide in or which religion you are a part of, as long as you truly believe. They say, "It doesn't matter what you believe, as long as you really believe it." Sadly, people today believe in all sorts of strange things. For example, Shirley McClaine abides in new age mysticism. While she is abiding in a vine, it's a false vine. Many people are very religious—counting beads, confessing sins, and following strict traditions—yet without Jesus Christ, they are abiding in false vines.

Jesus' claims in this passage and throughout the New Testament were exclusive. He basically excluded every religious "way to Heaven" and claimed to be the only truth, the only life, the only Saviour. Jesus stepped forward on history's pages and said, *"I am the true vine."*

In this parable, the branches represent the lives of believers—people who share life from the Vine. Friend, do you know for sure that you are fixed to the true Vine? Have you trusted Jesus Christ as your only Saviour? He invites you to come to Him in faith and to place one hundred percent of your trust in Him to forgive your sins and take you to Heaven. He is the only way! I pray you will settle this important decision as you continue to read.

I thank God that the Vine from which I draw my strength and sustenance is Jesus Christ, the Son of God, the Creator of the world. He lived a perfectly sinless life on this earth, died on a cross for my sins, and rose again for my justification. What a privilege to enter into a personal relationship with Him—to accept His invitation to abide in Him!

His presence is supreme—to abide with Jesus Christ is to abide with God Himself. There is no other religion that can offer this kind of wonderful relationship.

The Invitation to His Presence

In verse four the Bible says, "*Abide in me, and I in you.*" He is inviting us into His presence. Understand this—before you can abide with someone, you must first enter into a relationship. Before you can abide in your home, you must first enter into that home. The way to enter into a relationship with Jesus Christ is by faith in His finished work.

Ephesians 2:8 tells us, "*For by grace are ye saved through faith; and that not of yourselves: it is the gift of God.*" Abiding in Christ begins by putting faith in Jesus Christ—trusting His death and resurrection for the payment of your sins. When you make this decision, the Bible says you are saved, and from that moment on, you can abide with Him in a personal relationship.

The invitation to His presence begins with salvation. Once you enter into that relationship, Jesus invites you to abide with Him. He invites you to come alongside of Him, draw sustenance from Him, and cling to Him like the branches cling to the vine. This relationship is not temporary—it is a lifelong journey.

After salvation, how do we continue to abide in Jesus Christ? One way to abide is through consistent time spent in the Bible. In John 1:1 the Bible says, "*In the beginning was the Word, and the Word was with God, and the Word was God.*" When you spend time in God's Word, you are spending time in God's presence. You are abiding with Him. His Word is alive and powerful and will change your life as you allow its truth to flow into your heart.

We can abide with the Lord through prayer. James 4:8 says, "*Draw nigh to God, and He will draw nigh to you....*" God invites you to come boldly into His presence and to ask according to His will. He desires to hear and answer your prayers today.

We can also abide in Christ through trials. In 1 Peter 1:7, the Bible is clear that the trials of our faith can become very precious if they draw us closer to God: "*That the trial of your faith, being much more precious than of gold that perisheth, though it be tried with fire, might be found unto praise and honour and glory at the appearing of Jesus Christ."* People who do not have the Lord often turn to alcohol, drugs, sin, and vice to cope with the hardships of life, but we can turn to a more intimate, close walk with the Lord. We can know that He is our Comforter and that He understands our burdens and trials.

In the old western days, a man was walking down the road carrying a bag of grain on his shoulder. Another man was riding along the road in a buckboard pulled by a horse. He came up beside the man carrying the grain and said, "Jump up here on the buckboard with me. It's too hot to be walking today." The man said, "Thank you," and got up onto the seat with his grain still on his shoulder. After a while, the driver said, "Why don't you put that grain down and relax?" The passenger said, "Oh, no. It's enough that you would allow me to ride—I would never ask you to carry my load, too!"

This is what many Christians do. They say, "Lord, I know You can save me, forgive my sins, and give me a home in Heaven, but I wouldn't ask You to carry my load too!" Friend, He said, "I want to abide with you. I want to carry your load and be your life." First Peter 5:7 tells us, *"Casting all your care upon him; for he careth for you."*

Jesus continues His statement, *"abide in me,"* in John 15:4, *"…and I in you."* How can Jesus Christ abide in you? He abides in you through His Holy Spirit. In Galatians 2:20, Paul said, *"…Christ liveth in me…"* When you received Christ as your Saviour, God's Holy Spirit came into your life.

John described His abiding in 1 John 2:27, *"…the anointing which ye have received of him abideth in you…"* The anointing we receive of the Lord is the Holy Spirit of God. So when Jesus says, "Abide in me and I will abide in you," He is referring to His Spirit who abides in us every moment of every day until we meet the

Lord. That is why Jesus Christ alone can say, *"...I will never leave thee, nor forsake thee"* (Hebrews 13:5).

The Consolation of His Presence

This truth is one of my favorites from this passage. John 15:9 says, *"As the Father hath loved me, so have I loved you: continue ye in my love."* The consolation of abiding in the Lord is His love. We live in a world that is starving for love. Yet, in this verse, Jesus invites us to abide with Him so that we might experience His powerful love. What a promise—"I'm going to love you as the Father loves Me."

The kind of love Jesus offers is very different from the world's love. It is eternal. First John 4:10 says, *"Herein is love, not that we loved God, but that he loved us..."* God loved you before you were ever born. God loved you before the foundation of the world. Jesus Christ loves you with an everlasting and limitless love. It is not based on your performance, your perfection, or your power to earn it! God loves you because He created you, and He desires for you to personally experience that love as you abide with Him in a close relationship.

God's love is also perfect. It is unconditional and totally accepting. First John 4:18 says, *"...perfect love casteth out fear...."* Earthly love often has fear attached to it: "I'll love you if you get straight *A*'s." "I'll love you if you make a touchdown." "I'll love you if you cook my dinner." "I'll love you if you bring home a paycheck." Some fear is always built into human love. We fear being rejected or not being accepted. But the Bible says, *"Perfect love casteth out fear."* God's love gives complete security in the presence of Jesus Christ. You don't have to fear whether or not He loves you or accepts you. His perfect love casts out fear.

God's love is unchanging. It is a love that will go on forever! Nothing can separate you from this wonderful love! You cannot do anything that would cause God to not love you! No power on earth can pull you out of His hand! He will never "change His mind" about you! He loves you with all of His heart—today and forever! In Romans 8:35, Paul said it this way, *"Who shall separate us from the love of Christ...?"* He continues in verses 38–39, *"For I am persuaded, that neither death, nor life, nor angels, nor principalities, nor powers, nor things present, nor things to come, Nor height, nor depth, nor any other creature, shall be able to separate us from the love of God, which is in Christ Jesus our Lord."* Friend, nothing will ever change God's love for you.

You may say, "I have done some bad things since I've been saved. I've had some problems and have made some mistakes." God still loves you. His love is unchanging, and His arms are open wide inviting you to return to Him in repentance. He waits to welcome you back into fellowship with Him, and though you have strayed from Him, His love remains steadfast for you.

Picture this. Jesus Christ is holding out His nail-pierced hands to you. He is saying to those who never put faith in Him, "Come to Me. Let Me be your Saviour. I am the true Vine." If you know Him, then He is saying to you, "Abide in Me. I am the supreme God. I invite you to know Me, and I desire to know you. I have an amazing love to give you that you cannot find anywhere else. Abide in Me, and let Me abide in you."

What a wonderful invitation from a wonderful Saviour! "Abide in Me. You have accepted Me, and I have accepted you. Walk with Me. Cling to Me. Settle down with Me. Just stay for a while with Me."

Will you respond to His invitation?

CHAPTER TWO

Abiding in His Purpose

J ohn Harper jostled his luggage while helping Nina, age six, with her suitcase. Harper was a Baptist minister in Glasgow on his way to a preaching engagement at the Moody Memorial Church of Chicago. His wife had died at Nina's birth, so he was traveling with his young daughter, assisted by Nina's aunt, Miss Jessie Leitch. After settling themselves in the second-class passenger section, they took off to roam the ship. They felt especially fortunate to be on the maiden voyage of the greatest ocean liner ever built—the *Titanic*.

This was not Harper's first brush with disaster. When he was two years old, he had fallen into a well and almost drowned. His mother rescued and resuscitated him by holding him by his heels while the water poured out of his lungs. When he was twenty-six, John was swimming in the ocean when he was caught by a riptide and barely fought his way back to shore. At age thirty-two, Harper found himself aboard a ship in the Mediterranean Sea that was taking on water so rapidly that the crew gave themselves up for dead.

He bore other difficulties as well. In the summer of 1905, his health broke under the strain of his pastoral labors, and friends grew alarmed at his thin frame and sallow complexion. The next year, his wife Annie died, leaving him with tiny Nina.

But Harper was a man of deep faith. "The fear of death did not for one moment disturb me," he said after one of his narrow escapes. "I believed that sudden death would be sudden glory."

John Harper was born into a Christian home on May 29, 1872, and converted at age thirteen. By age eighteen, he knew God had a special mission for him. Though working at the local paper mill, John found himself preaching the Gospel to whoever would listen, often standing on street corners after work and proclaiming Christ.

After several years of personal evangelism and street preaching, he was recruited by the Baptists to oversee one of their struggling mission works. Here Harper labored for thirteen years, watching the church grow from twenty-five members to over five hundred and building a sanctuary that could seat nine hundred. He was known for his intense prayer life. Some nights he would stay at church all night, pleading with God for his hundreds of members by name.

In 1910, Harper was called to Walworth Road Church in London where his preaching skills flourished. The church there grew quickly and souls were added to the Kingdom.

Then came an invitation from the Moody Memorial Church of Chicago to preach a special winter series of messages. Harper made the trip with great excitement, and the Lord so blessed his ministry there that he was hardly home when the Moody Church contacted him again, pleading for him to return for a second series of services.

It was a hard decision, for his London flock didn't want to lose their pastor for another three months. One man, Mr. Robert English, pleaded with Harper not to make the trip, saying that while in prayer he had felt an ominous impression of impending disaster. He offered to pay for a new ticket if only Harper would delay his trip. But Harper felt compelled to go. He boarded the *Titanic* on April 10, 1912.

Four nights into the voyage, Harper stood on deck admiring the sunset. "It will be beautiful in the morning," he said. He was seen later in the evening witnessing to a man; then he went to bed.

In the wee hours of the morning, he was jolted awake as the *Titanic* plowed into a massive iceberg. Quickly wrapping Nina in a blanket, he carried her to the deck and secured a place for her on a lifeboat. When the ship sank, Nina was saved in lifeboat number eleven, sitting on her aunt's lap. For many years, she would not speak of that night, but before her death in 1986, she told of remembering the lights of the ship going out and hearing the screams of the dying.

But what of her father?

Harper took off his life jacket and gave it to another man, shouting, "Let the women, children, and the unsaved into the lifeboats!" When the *Titanic* sank, he tumbled into the freezing waters where he perished.

Months later, in a church in Hamilton, Canada, a man rose, saying, "I was on the *Titanic* the night she went down. I was thrown into the waters and managed to grab a spar and hang on for dear life. The waters were icy. Suddenly, a wave brought a man near, John Harper of Glasgow. He too was holding to a piece of wreckage. He called out, 'Man, are you saved?'

'No, I am not,' I replied.

He shouted back through the darkness, 'Believe on the Lord Jesus Christ, and thou shalt be saved.'

The waves bore him away, but a little later he was washed back alongside me. 'Are you saved now?' he called out.

'No,' I replied.

'Believe on the Lord Jesus Christ, and thou shalt be saved.' Then losing his hold on the wood, he sank. And there, alone in the night with two miles of water under me, I trusted Christ as my Saviour. I am John Harper's last convert."

John Harper was a man who knew his purpose in life—to tell as many as he could about the love of God. Even in his final moments, he was leading others to the Saviour.

What about you?

Do you know the purpose for your existence? Are you abiding in that God-given purpose?

In John 14:30, the Lord indicated to His disciples that His earthly ministry would soon end and that He would not be able to physically walk with them or teach them much longer. Jesus prepared them as He spoke, *"Hereafter I will not talk much with you: for the prince of this world cometh, and hath nothing in me."* Jesus told them in John 14:17 that the Holy Spirit would come and indwell their lives soon after He was gone: *"Even the Spirit of truth; whom the world cannot receive, because it seeth him not, neither knoweth him: but ye know him; for he dwelleth with you, and shall be in you."*

As a Christian, you can abide in Christ and know God's leading in your life day by day through the indwelling of His Holy Spirit. It is a great joy to abide in the person of Christ—to know that His Spirit is with you each moment. If you are a Christian, He is with you every minute of every day.

At the office—He is with you.

At the store—He is with you.

At the emergency room—He is with you.

Even while doing the laundry or making breakfast—He promises to be with you and to never leave you or forsake you.

The more you abide in His *person*, the greater the desire will grow in your life to fulfill His *purpose*. The more you abide in Him, the more you learn of Him. You cannot come into contact with Christ, be saved, and not have your purpose in life completely transformed. In fact, Paul said that Timothy had been called according to the purpose of God. In a greater sense, all believers have been called according to the purpose of God.

You have been saved for a reason. God has a purpose for your life, and it is up to you to live it! Have you ever come to a place in your life when you could say, "Lord, I no longer want to live life for my gratification, my pursuits, my ambitions. I want to have *Your* purpose flowing through me, so I may bring forth the fruit of Your presence"? Knowing and fulfilling God's purposes is one of the greatest joys of the Christian life.

The Purpose of the Abiding Christian

What is the purpose of life for someone who is abiding in Christ? John 15:2 tells us, *"Every branch in me that beareth not fruit he taketh away: and every branch that beareth fruit, he purgeth it, that it may bring forth more fruit."*

The purpose of a Christian's life is that he might bear fruit through an abiding relationship with Jesus Christ. The Bible says in verse 16 of the same chapter, *"Ye have not chosen me, but I have chosen you, and ordained you, that ye should go and bring forth fruit, and that your fruit should remain…."*

God makes it very clear that the purpose of our lives is to bear fruit—fruit that remains. The purpose of your church is to bear fruit as well. How are you doing? Are you bearing fruit? Titus 3:14 says, *"And let ours also learn to maintain good works for necessary uses, that they be not unfruitful."* Paul exhorted Titus to make sure that the believers were not unfruitful. Paul wanted to remind them of their responsibility to bear fruit.

The Bible explains this in Psalm 1:1–3, *"Blessed is the man that walketh not in the counsel of the ungodly, nor standeth in the way of sinners, nor sitteth in the seat of the scornful. But his delight is in the law of the LORD ; and in his law doth he meditate day and night. And he shall be like a tree planted by the rivers of water, that bringeth forth his fruit in his season; his leaf also shall not wither; and whatsoever he doeth shall prosper."*

When you are planted in the Lord Jesus Christ, the natural result is to bear spiritual fruit. Someone who is truly born again, who lives next to the waters of Jesus Christ and the Word of God, will bear fruit. A Christian's very purpose for existence is to bear fruit.

If you have never lived in a desert, you may not understand this, but I promise it's true: the color green is very rare in the desert! If you want anything to survive in the desert you must have a method of daily watering.

I can remember moving to the sweltering high desert of Southern California from beautiful, lush Northern California. It was my second summer living in the Antelope Valley, and I decided it was time to plant some grass in my backyard. My goal was *green* grass.

One day, my neighbor came over and said, "Just some advice—if you are going to plant anything in that backyard, you better make sure you put in a sprinkler system." Coming from Northern California where there was a little more humidity, a sprinkler system was more of an option.

I kindly thanked him for his advice and assured him that I would water it daily by hand. I did not have the time, money, or patience to install a sprinkler system, so I just watered it by hand every day.

A month or two had passed, and we had to leave town for a couple days. Upon our return, I walked into the backyard just in time to view the devastation. The color green was nowhere to be found! I couldn't believe it! Only two days had elapsed. My beautiful backyard had turned into a forgotten cemetery of browns and yellows.

I learned something that day—you need irrigation systems in the desert. As surely as grass in a desert needs water, not once in a while, but every day, so you and I must abide daily in Christ if we will bear fruit.

The purpose of the abiding Christian is to bear fruit. Whenever there is a lack of fruitfulness in your life, it is indicative of a lack of abiding in the Word of God—the rivers of Living Water. Abiding in His person will lead you to know and fulfill His purpose for your life. Psalm 92:13–14 says, *"Those that be planted in the house of the LORD shall flourish in the courts of our God. They shall still bring forth fruit in old age; they shall be fat and flourishing."*

Some that are elderly may think, "I'm too old to bear fruit. I've done my part." That is not what the text indicates. The Bible teaches that when we are planted in the Word of God and in the house of the Lord, we will bring forth fruit in our old age. We will be flourishing as a spiritual vine, bearing fruit. If God were finished helping you to produce fruit, He would take you home to Heaven. The very fact that you are alive is evidence that God wants *you* to produce fruit.

We are not left on earth merely to make money, live in a nice home, drive a nice automobile, or have a comfortable retirement one day. We are here to produce fruit that pleases Jesus Christ.

The Product of an Abiding Christian

The Fruit of the Spirit

Fruit bearing in the Bible involves more than leading people to Jesus Christ. That is a small part of a bigger picture. Fruit bearing is Christ-likeness. If Christ is the Vine and we are the branches, then our fruit is Christ-likeness.

What does the term *fruit* specifically mean? There are two definitions for *fruit bearing* that are found in the Bible. First, there is the fruit of the Spirit. If God's Spirit flows through you like sap flowing from the vine to the branches, you will bear fruit in your Christian character. Much like the trees in the spring produce leaves and fruit, our lives should produce fruit through the Holy Spirit. Galatians 5:22–23 says, *"But the fruit of the Spirit is love, joy, peace, longsuffering, gentleness, goodness, faith, Meekness, temperance: against such there is no law."*

What are some evidences of a fruitful life? Is a Spirit-filled, fruit-bearing life all about emotional display, speaking in tongues, or other sensational manifestations? No. This fruit of the Spirit goes far beyond getting excited in a worship service. It deals with the way you live your life everyday.

One of the evidences of the Spirit is a God-like love. Only God can grow this in your life. It is the kind of love we read about in 1 Corinthians 13—the kind that endures all things. Christians who are easily offended show through their impatience that they are not filled with the Holy Spirit of God. Their lovelessness is evidence they are not abiding in Jesus Christ. The fruit of the Spirit is love—it endures all things.

Another fruit of the Spirit is joy. This is not the world's happiness. Instead, it is an inner spiritual joy bubbling up from Jesus Christ.

The fruit of the Spirit is also peace. Peace is a tranquility of mind that comes from God, not from pills. This is the peace of God that brings stability and strength to our lives no matter what the circumstances of life are dictating.

The fruit of the Spirit is longsuffering, which means steadfastness under pressure. Have you ever stopped to observe two people going through a similar trial at the same time? One man may be facing unemployment and having family problems, yet he continues to attend church and remains faithful to his family and to God. He manages to have a sweet spirit toward others as well.

The next man, enduring similar trials, becomes disgusted with the church, his family, and sometimes even God. He no longer has a compliant spirit. He is bitter at his circumstances and angry with others.

Both claim to be Christians. What is the difference? Why is one man faithful and the other man bitter? The answer is that the joyful man is abiding in Jesus Christ, filled with the Holy Spirit of God. He is bearing the fruit that only God can give. He is longsuffering.

Another fruit of the Spirit is gentleness. This is a Holy Spirit generated kindness and ease that expresses care and compassion to others. Have you ever been around someone who is rough in his spirit? We would all rather be treated with gentleness.

The Spirit will also produce goodness—the opposite of evil. He will give you a desire for good things and cause you to love goodness more and hate sin more.

Have you ever desired to grow in your faith? That desire is another fruit that the Holy Spirit wants to produce in your life. He will develop, build, and strengthen your faith as you abide in Him.

Meekness is another fruit that the Holy Spirit will bear from within. Meekness is power under control. It is giving Christ the preeminence in your life and relationships. It is death to self and to the flesh, and it is the disposition of grace guiding my words, actions, and attitudes.

Finally, the Spirit will give you temperance—self-control. He will give you the strength and the grace to control your emotions, your spirit, and your desires.

The fruit of the Spirit is love, joy, peace, longsuffering, gentleness, goodness, faith, meekness, and temperance.

Randy had asked me many times to visit his wife, Victoria, who desperately needed Jesus. I was the new associate pastor at the time and eager for any chance to be a blessing to our church family. I went to his house the first chance I had. Together, we sat down with his wife.

Victoria sat directly across from me and made it clear the entire time I was there that I was not welcome. She sat anxiously puffing on her cigarette. Some people at least blow the smoke out the side of their mouth, but not Randy's wife. She blew smoke right into my face!

With her Budweiser in one hand and her cigarette in the other, I began talking to her about the love of God. If looks could kill, you would have had my funeral. She was not interested.

In the weeks to follow, Randy and I began praying earnestly for his wife to be saved. I asked the Holy Spirit to bear fruit through me, so that I might show love, joy, peace, and longsuffering toward this woman.

I will never forget watching her come into church that next Sunday morning. She came in, sat in the back, and glared at the preacher the entire service. People have a way of using body language to let you know what they think about their surroundings. Her body language said, "I don't want to be here!"

As the preacher preached, I began to watch her throughout the service. I sensed the Spirit of God starting to tug at her heart. She came forward, and one of the ladies took her to a counseling room where she accepted Jesus Christ as her Saviour!

I wish you could meet this lady today. I wish you could see the fruit of the Spirit in her life. I wish you could see how God uses this lady every week to bring others to Jesus Christ. I wish you could watch how she raises her family in church each week and stands by her husband in ministry. I wish you could see what has happened in her life.

The difference was Jesus Christ. She put her faith in Jesus Christ, and today she is abiding in His person. She now has a new purpose for living, and that purpose is to bear the fruit of the Lord in her life.

The Fruit of Soulwinning

The second type of fruit bearing is bringing others to Jesus Christ. Proverbs 11:30 says, *"The fruit of the righteous is a tree of life; and he that winneth souls is wise."* An apple tree bears apples, an orange tree bears oranges, and a Christian bears more Christians.

Soulwinning is reproducing other Christians. You cannot abide in Jesus Christ without having a desire to see other people saved. It is a part of your spiritual growth.

I remember when our oldest daughter, Danielle, was saved. She was five years old. I will never forget the day following her salvation. I noticed her over in a corner sort of sulking and teary eyed. I asked her, "Sweetheart, what's wrong?" She said, "Larry's not saved yet, Dad. Larry needs to get saved." She wanted her younger brother to be saved.

Nearly every time someone gets saved, the response brought forth by the Holy Spirit is a desire to share the Gospel with someone else. Allow the Holy Spirit to plant the seed of fruit bearing in your life.

Psalm 126:5–6 says, *"They that sow in tears shall reap in joy. He that goeth forth and weepeth, bearing precious seed, shall doubtless come again with rejoicing, bringing his sheaves with him."* The fruit of the Spirit will affect your temperament, your personality, and your response to everyday situations. You will see others as souls in need of a Saviour, and you will have a burden to tell them of the love of Christ.

The *purpose* of the abiding Christian is to bear fruit. The *product* of the abiding Christian is the fruit of the Holy Spirit and the salvation of lost souls.

The Praise of the Abiding Christian

The praise of the abiding Christian is found in John 15:8, *"Herein is my Father glorified, that ye bear much fruit; so shall ye be my disciples."*

A Christian who abides in Christ will bring glory to God. Our praise will be deflected to the Heavenly Father: *"Herein is my Father glorified."* Understand that the chief end of man is to glorify God. We bear fruit to glorify Him. If a soul receives Christ, if a church gets built, if something good happens—to God be the glory for what He has done!

The praise of the abiding Christian always goes to the Heavenly Father. We do not win souls, give offerings, or serve Christ so we can glorify ourselves. We do it all for the glory of God.

Christian, our purpose in this life is to bear spiritual fruit. James said, *"Faith without works is dead."*

John Harper knew his purpose in life. He evidenced it by the love he had for his daughter, and by his concern for the lost around him. The fruit of the Spirit fell from his branches that frigid day. A man was watching Mr. Harper and was saved as a result of his testimony.

Will you also choose to abide in His purpose for your life?

CHAPTER THREE

Abiding in His Purging

On May 8, 1984, Benjamin M. Weir, veteran Presbyterian missionary to Lebanon, was kidnapped at gunpoint by Shiite Muslims in Beirut. During his sixteen-month imprisonment, he was constantly threatened with death. On his first night in captivity, one of his abductors commanded him to face the wall, which he did. "Now take your blindfold off and put this on." The man handed Benjamin a pair of ski goggles with the eye-holes covered with thick, black tape. All light was completely obliterated. In Weir's mind, the sun had set. He later wrote:

> In the twilight there came to my mind the hymn, *Abide with Me, Fast Falls the Eventide.* I felt vulnerable, helpless, and lonely. I felt tears in my eyes. Then I remembered the promise of Jesus, "*If ye abide in me, and my words abide in you, ye shall ask what ye will, and it shall be done unto you.*" And so I prayed, "Lord, I remember Your promise, and I think it applies to

me, too. I've done nothing to deserve it but receive it as a free gift. I need You. I need Your assurance and guidance to be faithful to You in this situation. Teach me what I need to learn. Deliver me from this place and this captivity if it is Your will. If it is not Your will to set me free, help me to accept whatever is involved. Show me Your gifts, and enable me to recognize them as coming from You. Praise be to You."

For the next sixteen months, Benjamin Weir's hope and joy was found in the fact that he was not simply abiding in captivity; he was abiding in Christ, and thus able to "bear much fruit." The words of this somber hymn came to comfort him during the darkest hours of his incarceration.

Abide with me! Fast falls the eventide.
The darkness deepens; Lord, with me abide!
When other helpers fail and comforts flee,
Help of the helpless, oh, abide with me!

For a Christian to "bear much fruit," he must be willing to accept the Master's purging. No one ever wants purging, but everyone wants fruit. Yet, purging is a necessary part of the fruit-bearing process.

For instance, nearly everyone has a favorite fruit and most everyone knows where to find that fruit. You walk into the store. You choose it. You pay for it. You take it home. You eat it.

But fruit doesn't just appear at the local grocery store. There is a process involved with planting, watering, cultivating, growing, harvesting, and transporting the fruit from the orchard to the shelf. So it is in the Christian life. Fruit does not just appear in the life of a Christian; it is grown through a process.

According to the words of Jesus, if a child of God is going to bear spiritual fruit, he must be willing to endure the rigors of growth. He must view every obstacle as an opportunity to reach his full potential as a Christian.

For growth to occur, two key contributors must be in place. First, you must receive the life-giving water of the Word of God. The psalmist said in Psalm 1:3 (speaking of the righteous man), *"And he shall be like a tree planted by the rivers of water, that bringeth forth his fruit in his season; his leaf also shall not wither; and whatsoever he doeth shall prosper."* How utterly foolish it would be for one to think that a tree could live without water, and yet it is even more absurd to think of someone trying to bear fruit apart from God's Word. You must be planted in a church where the water of the Word of God runs freely, and you must spend time daily in God's Word to satisfy your need for spiritual nourishment.

Second, you must have spiritual receptivity—an open and submissive heart toward the Word of God. The Bible speaks of this in Matthew 13:23, *"But he that received seed into the good ground is he that heareth the word, and understandeth it; which also beareth fruit, and bringeth forth, some an hundredfold, some sixty, some thirty."* Jesus likened those who received the Word of God on good ground to a withered flower receiving a cool rain on a summer day. Their minds were receptive. Their hearts were open. Like a farmer prepares his land by plowing, a Christian must prepare his heart by choosing to be tender to the Word of God.

Jesus was very clear in Luke 6:38 when He said, *"Give, and it shall be given unto you; good measure, pressed down, and shaken together, and running over, shall men give into your bosom. For with the same measure that ye mete withal it shall be measured to you again."* People who leave a church will often use the excuse, "I left because I just wasn't getting anything out of it." Inherent in their statement is that they were not putting anything into it.

The Bible principle remains true, *"Give, and it shall be given unto you."* You will receive in direct proportion to your preparation. How much time do you take to prepare your heart before a church service? What kind of "ground" does the seed of God's Word fall upon in your life? Hosea was accurate when he admonished the children of Israel in Hosea 10:12, *"Sow to yourselves in righteousness, reap in mercy; break up your fallow ground: for it is time to seek the LORD, till he come and rain righteousness upon you."*

If a Christian is going to bear fruit, from time to time there will be purging that is orchestrated by the Heavenly Father. There will be a process of pruning. It is not always pleasant, nor is it always at the time we would choose. But there must be trimming, there must be shaping, there must be chastising by a loving Heavenly Father for us to experience the abundant fruit of an abiding relationship.

A man completely dejected by life's afflictions was walking one day in the botanical gardens of Oxford when a fine pomegranate tree caught his eye. One of the stems had been cut deeply with a pruning knife. Upon asking the gardener the reason, he received an answer that shed new light on his troubled soul.

"Sir," said the gardener, "This tree used to shoot up and out so strongly that it bore nothing but leaves. Therefore, I was obligated to cut it in this manner, and when it was almost cut through, then it began to bear plenty of fruit."

Webster defines *purging* this way: "to make free of impurities, to rid of unfriendly elements." God the Heavenly Father is very concerned about anything in our lives that is "unfriendly" to Him. If there is pride, He wants to purge it. If there is hurt, He wants to heal it. If there are burdens, He wants to bear them. God desires for you to bear fruit. Even in purging, He is preparing you for greater blessings and victories.

In our text, Jesus Christ is the Vine. We as believers are the branches. It is interesting that of all of the plants God could have chosen to illustrate this truth, He chose the vine and the branch. If you have ever had time to observe grape vines, you will notice that the branches are prone to wander. The vine stays fairly taut, but the branches like to run. The shooters like to spread out. They have a mind of their own. They are full of freedom, and they go where they want to go, do what they want to do, and sometimes they anchor into wasteful soil. Sometimes they run into areas where they should not be, and there is the need for a husbandman to prune the branches.

You and I are like those branches, prone to wander, wanting to do our will, ready to do what we want when we want. Jesus is the Vine, and God is the good Husbandman. His gentle hands prune and purge areas of our lives that have gone astray. His guiding touch draws us back to the true Vine desiring to keep us anchored to Christ and bearing good fruit.

There are three reasons why we should patiently abide in Christ during times of purging.

Purging Signifies the Providence of God

Purging reminds us of God's divine intervention. He has gone before us with His will. He is sovereign. He has a plan for our lives, and He is in control.

Jesus, speaking to His eleven disciples, said in John 15:1, *"I am the true vine, and my Father is the husbandman."* A husbandman is a vine-dresser. He has all authority over the branches. Like a father who knows what is best for a child, God the Father knows what is best for us.

A little boy who plays out in the middle of the street is acting against his father's will. That father will go to his son, bring him back into the house, and reprove him through loving discipline. Our Heavenly Father does the same. He loves us too much to let us stray into danger. When we become prone to wander and run from His will, He brings us back to the safety of an abiding relationship with Christ.

The Bible refers to this in Hebrews 12:6–8, *"For whom the Lord loveth he chasteneth, and scourgeth every son whom he receiveth. If ye endure chastening, God dealeth with you as with sons; for what son is he whom the father chasteneth not? But if ye be without chastisement, whereof all are partakers, then are ye bastards, and not sons."*

A Christian who resists the Holy Spirit by repeatedly saying "no" to God and by repeatedly refusing to yield his own will is forcing God to purge his life. The Husbandman may take a branch away from the Vine, if He chooses. No church can do that, no individual can do that, but the Husbandman can do that. This doesn't mean the loss of salvation, but it can mean literal removal from this earth. If a person resists the Holy Spirit and bears no fruit, then he is missing his very purpose for living. God desires for every Christian to bear fruit and glorify Him.

The Bible goes on to say in John 15:2, *"…Every branch that beareth fruit, he purgeth it…."* It is easy to assume that an individual living for himself would need some pruning, but here the Bible is referring to someone who is already fruitful! These are the Christians who are faithfully going to church, singing in the choir, teaching a Sunday school class, bringing a new family to church, and sincerely living for Christ. Yes, even faithful, godly Christians need God's purging.

This purging may not be chastisement, but it is nevertheless God's way of shaping us and molding us to His will. The Lord can prune even a faithful branch. You may be doing your best to serve God, but you can still come under this type of a pruning process. When you face hardship, remember that God only prunes for your profit, your betterment, your productivity. He purges so that you can bear more fruit.

Robert Browning Hamilton said it wisely when he wrote:

> I walked a mile with Pleasure;
> She chatted all the way;

But left me none the wiser
For all she had to say.

I walked a mile with Sorrow,
And ne'er a word said she;
But, oh! The things I learned from her,
When sorrow walked with me.

Sometimes the vocabulary of pleasure depends on the imagery of pain. At times, we rejoice. At times, we weep. But never do we see more clearly than through eyes that are washed with tears.

When we abide during times of purging, we are saying, just like Benjamin Weir, "God, I don't like the way this feels. I don't like the trials I am having right now, but I'm going to acknowledge that You are God. And, I'm going to let You do what You need to do in my life. After all, You are the Husbandman. You are the One who is in control of my life."

Purging Increases the Productivity of God's People

The Bible says, "...*He purgeth it, that it may bring forth more fruit*" (vs. 2). God says to a Christian who is serious about bearing fruit, "If there is anything that is drawing your affection, if there is anything between you and Me, I need to purge it from your life for you to bear more fruit." By removing the object of affection, God is now able to produce fruit more freely.

If you have ever seen a productive vineyard, then you know the branches need to be tautly held to the vine. God intends for us to remain attached to Him during our times of trials and afflictions. Some of the most fruitful Christians are those who have stayed faithful through the most difficult trials that life has to offer. They clung to the Vine—Jesus Christ. They grew stronger. Now, they are producing greater fruit in their lives.

Yet, the Christian who turns his back on God during times of purging is the Christian who has another trial awaiting him and another lesson to be learned.

That is why Paul could say in Romans 5:3–5, *"And not only so, but we glory in tribulations also: knowing that tribulation worketh patience; And patience, experience; and experience, hope: And hope maketh not ashamed; because the love of God is shed abroad in our hearts by the Holy Ghost which is given unto us."*

The Apostle Paul was able to praise God in his tribulations. Can you do that? Paul realized that as he was going through the tribulations and the difficult times, God was placing patience and hope within him. Through that trial, God was teaching him something that he could have never learned in a Sunday school class, in a Bible college, or in a Sunday service.

This is why Paul could later spring to his feet and say, *"For I am not ashamed of the gospel of Christ…"* (Romans 1:16). God was teaching him that, through the burdens, come the blessings. Through purging comes greater productivity.

Do you desire to bear greater fruit for Christ? Are you willing to endure the present purging, so you can fulfill a greater purpose? Friend, let the strength of Christ flow into your heart through your abiding relationship. The purging you face now will only yield a greater reward when harvest time comes!

Purging Facilitates the Purification of God's People

Jesus said in John 15:3, *"Now ye are clean through the word which I have spoken unto you."* Here the Lord Jesus was speaking to His eleven disciples. Perhaps, as He spoke these words, He had a vineyard in His view. Jesus was preparing them for His impending death, burial, and resurrection. He was very interested at this point in their being *clean* or set apart for the task at hand.

As He spoke to them, He was using two different applications. In one, He spoke to the group, and in the other, He spoke to individuals. They had been cleansed as a group by the words that Jesus spoke and probably by the removal of Judas from their midst. Judas was the one who had the outward appearance of belief, but who had never truly put his faith in Jesus Christ. As a result, he was removed from their midst. Sometimes, God will purge a group or a church, and there will be those who are removed by the providence of God.

God is also concerned with our individual spiritual purity. He desires that we keep short accounts with Him and that we regularly confess and forsake sin.

Purging is a part of God's purification process. His Word is a cleansing agent. His Word is a pruning tool to mold us into the image of Christ. The Bible says in Hebrews 4:12, "*For the word of God is quick, and powerful, and sharper than any twoedged sword, piercing even to the dividing asunder of soul and spirit, and of the joints and marrow, and is a discerner of the thoughts and intents of the heart.*"

The Word of God is quick—it is alive—and it enters our lives with power to cleanse and purify us before God. Why does God's Word purify us? Because purging always produces more fruit. Remember that God has a purpose for purging. He desires us to be pure vessels, bearing fruit that pleases Him.

Perhaps you are experiencing some great burden. Perhaps you are in the midst of some great trial. If you've been running from God and His purging has brought chastisement, turn back to the Lord today.

If God is trying to touch your life now and bring you closer to the Vine, Jesus Christ, then bend willingly at the touch of God and simply say, "God, I acknowledge to You that I'm just a branch, and You are the Vine. I acknowledge that You are the Husbandman.

If this trial in my life is meant to draw me closer to Jesus, then I accept it and I claim Your grace to see me through."

This is what Peter meant when he spoke of the trial of faith in 1 Peter 1:7, *"That the trial of your faith, being much more precious than of gold that perisheth, though it be tried with fire, might be found unto praise and honour and glory at the appearing of Jesus Christ."* If you abide in Christ through times of purging, one day, you will be able to praise and thank God for His goodness in your life when you see Him face to face.

In James 1:4, James encouraged the Christians at Jerusalem not to run during times of purging: *"But let patience have her perfect work, that ye may be perfect and entire, wanting nothing."* Often during trials we are tempted to turn away from God and return to old friends and old lifestyles. We are tempted to return to sinful and fleshly habits. Instead of abiding faithfully in the Word of God, keeping a sensitive heart, and abiding in Jesus Christ, we are tempted to withdraw from God. As a result, we limit God's potential work in our hearts. God will not force His work in you. You must allow it. Yet, when you run from God during a time of purging, you are restricting the eventual fruit bearing that He would have produced in your life!

I was visiting my mother and father-in-law's home one evening when God taught me a very important lesson. Immediately upon my arrival, I was escorted out to the garden in the backyard. If you visited my father-in-law during gardening season, you did not greet his wife, you did not meet the dog, and you did not sit down and talk—you went straight to the garden!

Usually, he would begin to show me row after row of beets and lettuce. He would talk of when he planted the seed and what kind of fertilizer he used. I always enjoyed every minute of it. I love gardens, and I love seeing new life grow.

That particular evening, the weather was cold, and every plant in the garden had been harvested. We walked around the corner of the house where the peach tree used to be. Only now I noticed it was not much of a peach tree. In fact, it was nothing but a three foot stub sticking out of the ground. I said emphatically, "Dad, you killed that thing!" He simply said, "No, that tree wasn't producing fruit. I called my friend up in Fresno, California, and he said there was only one thing to do with a tree like that—whack it right down to the ground."

It was like going into the barber shop and asking for a little trim and getting a Marine haircut in return. I didn't want to argue with him, because I didn't want him whacking me down to the ground! In my heart, I thought, "That thing's dead. There is no way that tree is ever going to recover."

Just a few summers later, I went by and took a look in that backyard. You'll never guess what I saw. The most fruitful peach tree I have ever seen. Why? Because purging had taken place, and greater fruit was the result.

God's plan for our earthly lives is not over until the trumpet sounds. Life's mishaps and tragedies are not a reason to bail out or to run from God. They are simply reasons to stay faithful and hopeful. They are reasons to abide and wait for greater fruit bearing.

When the train goes through a tunnel and the world gets dark, do you jump out? Of course not. You sit still and trust the engineer to get you through.

How do you deal with purging? What is the cure for pruning?

The answer is found in abiding in Jesus Christ. You aren't the first person to weep. You aren't the first person to need help. God is still on His throne. Your day to bloom is just around the corner. Sit still. Abide. Trust the Engineer to see you through the tunnel. Greater fruit is just ahead in your life.

CHAPTER FOUR

Abiding in Prayer

"Good morning, Lord. I present myself to You today as a living sacrifice. I am here to serve You and to obey Your orders. What would You like for me to do today?"

What if this became your prayer? What if every day, you reenlisted into the service of the King? How differently would your day operate?

We know a lot about prayer, we talk a lot about prayer, but we don't pray. The need of every church, every preacher, and every family is not a seminar on prayer, books on prayer, better prayer stationary, or promising to pray. We need to pray! Prayer is how we lay hold on the blessings and the power of God. Like the old *Nike* slogan—Just Do It!

Throughout the Scriptures, God indicates His desire for us to commune with Him in prayer. God shows us His willingness to help us when we have needs or problems. Does your life more closely resemble a "crisis-management" mentality or a "prayer-dependent" mentality?

It has been my experience that many Christians are good at praying when others are around, but they often don't have a personal, private time with the Lord. Praying for a meal or an offering can almost be effortless, but personal, private prayer in an abiding relationship can be a daunting task. Yet, if you intend to truly have an abiding relationship with Jesus Christ, you must learn to abide with Him in prayer. You must learn to spend time with Him—praising, pleading, and interceding on behalf of others.

Let's discover how we can abide in Christ through personal prayer.

The Preparation for Prayer

First Thessalonians 5:17 teaches us to *"pray without ceasing."* James 5:16, reminds us, *"…The effectual fervent prayer of a righteous man availeth much."* James says furthermore, in James 4:2, *"…yet ye have not, because ye ask not."* In Psalm 34:17, David reminds us, *"The righteous cry, and the LORD heareth, and delivereth them out of all their troubles."* God wants us to abide in prayer. God wants us to be able to bear the fruit of answered prayer in our lives.

How can we abide more effectively in prayer? Jesus answers this question throughout the Scriptures. He tells us, step by step, how we can maintain an abiding relationship with Him through prayer. He gives us several prerequisites to prepare us for prayer.

Praise the Lord

Our hearts should be set on the praise and adoration of God when we come to Him. When Jesus taught the disciples concerning prayer, He taught them this phrase: *"…Our Father which art in heaven, Hallowed be thy name"* (Matthew 6:9). More than just a repeated prayer, this was meant to be a pattern of prayer. If our hearts are going to be prepared for prayer, we need to understand the holiness and power of God, and we need to come to Him with sincere praise and honor.

We see this evidenced in Paul and Silas. Notice their testimony after being thrown into jail at Philippi: *"And at midnight Paul and Silas prayed, and sang praises unto God…"* (Acts 16:25). These were men whose hearts were filled with praise for their God. Praising God is the preparation for a successful prayer life.

Confess Known Sin

The Bible makes a striking statement in Psalm 66:18, *"If I regard iniquity in my heart, the Lord will not hear me."* If I hide unconfessed sin in my heart, the Lord says He will not hear me. To have a successful prayer life we need to come clean with God and confess our sins to Him. Anything less is a mere show. God already knows every sin we have committed. We can't "put on a front" with Him. When you begin your time with God, you should enter His presence, acknowledge your sin, and seek His forgiveness. Make sure you are right with God as you approach Him.

Exercise Faith

Matthew 21:22 says, *"And all things, whatsoever ye shall ask in prayer, believing, ye shall receive."* The word *believe* means "to put your total confidence in the Lord." God's Word promises us that when we pray in faith believing, we can receive the blessing of God. However, faith is not demanding something from God. Faith is not telling God what to do. Faith believes that God can do whatever He determines to do. Faith places total confidence in the power of God.

Pray in Jesus' Name

As we come to the Lord in prayer, we must remember to pray in the name of Jesus Christ. Jesus said in John 14:13, *"And whatsoever ye shall ask in my name, that will I do, that the Father may be glorified in the Son."* When we pray in Jesus' name, we invoke the authority of God. We are asking that His will be done.

Pray Persistently

Ephesians 6:18 says, *"Praying always with all prayer…."* In the Gospel of Luke, Jesus taught the disciples that there were certain prayer requests that were only going to be answered through importunity. Persistent prayer is more than just coming to God "once in a while." To abide in prayer, we must continually bombard the throne of grace with our requests.

Abide in His Word

Jesus said in John 15:7, *"If ye abide in me, and my words abide in you…."* Notice the word *if.* There is something we must first do before we can receive the promise. Romans 10:17 says, *"So then faith cometh by hearing, and hearing by the word of God."* Jesus says, "As you're preparing for a fruitful prayer life, you must first abide in Me, and My words must be abiding in you."

Friend, the Word of God should guide your prayer life. The more you mature in Christ, the more you will understand the Word of God, and the more your prayer life will be in sync with His will and desires.

For example, Proverbs 28:9 says, *"He that turneth away his ear from hearing the law, even his prayer shall be abomination."* If you are not heeding God's Word, your prayer request is a mockery to Him.

Perhaps you did this in school. Remember that subject you hated in junior high or high school? Remember how you didn't like the teacher, didn't like the lectures, didn't like the subject, and didn't listen in class? Then, when the test came, you probably begged God to help you pass! In the same way, God says, "When you reject My law and My instruction, your prayer is an abomination." God desires more than an "emergency-based relationship" with you.

Psalm 37:4 says, *"Delight thyself also in the LORD; and he shall give thee the desires of thine heart."* God doesn't want to withhold His blessing. He wants you to delight in His Word so that He may give you the desires of your heart.

As you prepare your heart daily for prayer, ask these questions: Am I abiding with Him now? Am I acknowledging His power and His presence? Am I praising His name? Have I confessed sin? Do I believe that He can answer this prayer? Am I praying in Jesus' name persistently? Am I staying in the Word of God faithfully? If you can answer these questions in the affirmative, you are ready to experience fruit in your prayer life.

The Definition of Prayer

Prayer is asking God for help. I realize we define prayer as talking to God, confessing sin, and adoring God, but the heart of prayer is simply asking God for help.

Matthew 7:7-8 says, *"Ask, and it shall be given you; seek, and ye shall find; knock, and it shall be opened unto you; For every one that asketh receiveth; and he that seeketh findeth; and to him that knocketh it shall be opened."* The Word of God teaches us that prayer is asking God. The Lord blesses our importunity—the fact that we continually come to Him with requests. God is pleased when we persistently ask Him for help.

Prayer is asking, but our asking must be subject to the will of God. If you are away from God and resisting His will, if you are dishonoring Him and denying His voice, then you are likely to ask for things that would not be good for you, and God has no obligation to hear your prayer.

In 2 Corinthians 12:8, the Apostle Paul asked the Lord three times for healing. In His will, the Lord didn't heal the apostle. In fact, the Lord said, "...*My grace is sufficient for thee....*" Sometimes, we will pray for things that are not in the will of God for us. He may choose not to heal or not to remove a burden. In these cases, He chooses to give a special measure of His sustaining grace—His strength—to carry us through the trial. This is why Paul was able to say in 2 Corinthians 12:9 "...*most gladly therefore will I rather glory in my infirmities....*" He said, "If God is going to give me grace and be glorified through all of this, I will just praise Him anyway."

You see, God is not a genie. Prayer is not my opportunity to tell Him what to do. Faith does not bind Him to my whims. Prayer is my privilege to seek His will and to ask for His help in accomplishing it.

James 4:3 tells us, "*Ye ask, and receive not, because ye ask amiss....*" Sometimes, we completely miss the mark in our prayer life. Like the man who prays, "God, I really need a new speed boat, and if You give me that boat, I'll only miss church two Sundays a month! God, I'll even have devotions on the boat." We like to strike up deals with God, don't we? Who do we really think we are to pray in such a way? You cannot pray against a biblical principle and expect God to bless!

James said our prayers are not answered because they are off the mark—they are out of the will of God. Friend, if you're not abiding in Christ, then most likely your prayers are focused on things that God doesn't desire for you. You could actually be praying dangerously!

The Manifestation of Prayer

What happens when people start praying? What happens when moms and dads and pastors and church members pray? John 15:7 says, "...*and it shall be done unto you.*" What an authoritative statement! If I meet the prerequisites that Jesus set forth, He simply says, *"It shall be done unto you!"*

The power of prayer is manifested by God's intervention in human affairs. I love to see God intervene in the lives of men. I believe one of the reasons God has blessed the Lancaster Baptist Church is because every Saturday night our men gather together and pray that God will bless our Sunday services. Week after week for more than twenty years, God has answered that prayer.

Think of Moses. Think of Gideon. Think of Hannah. Each of these came before God asking for help—seeking His provision and power. And every time, God honored their requests. He intervened in their lives with His mighty power!

William Carey, the great missionary to India, often said, "Attempt great things for God and expect great things from God." He was a man who had learned how to pray and believed that God could answer prayer. I'm glad I serve a God who specializes in impossible situations and mightily answers prayer.

Lancaster Baptist Church is a testimony of the power of prayer—nothing more and nothing less. When Terrie and I came to this church twenty years ago, we came with faith in God. God repeatedly intervened in our lives and provided food, a home, and money to pay the bills. As the church began to get on its feet, God continued to intervene and answer prayer. He has shown Himself mighty in thousands of ways to us over the years. Every victory in our ministry has been a prayer victory, and God has never failed us!

From starting our Christian school, to buying land, to building buildings, to starting West Coast Baptist College—every single victory was the result of God answering prayer. We stepped out in faith, trusted Him, and prayed that He would provide. In every case, God opened doors and intervened in miraculous ways.

In 1987, we were praying for a new church property. Our church was growing, and we believed that God wanted to give us a new location with room to expand. In 1988, we hosted a giving banquet for our small church family. The theme that night was "Giving by Faith"! Approximately fifty people gave $50,000 by faith that night. It was a historic miracle for our young church. The next day, a man approached me about a twenty-acre parcel of land that had just become available. Amazingly, we needed $50,000 for the down payment on that land. Coincidence? No! God was blessing our faith and answering our prayers! Today that twenty acres has become seventy-eight acres with dozens of buildings and thousands of church members and students being ministered to daily. God exceeded all that we could have asked or imagined in 1988!

This has been the story of Lancaster Baptist Church. God has powerfully manifested Himself by answered prayer!

Friend, there is no doubt you need God's help with something right now. You probably need answers to prayer, and God promises, "If you will abide in Me and my Word in you, you can ask what you will and it shall be done unto you."

Why would God be so available? Why would He care? Why is He so interested in answering your prayers? Jesus tells us in John 14:13, *"And whatsoever ye shall ask in my name, that will I do, that the Father may be glorified in the Son."*

Why does the Lord bless us? He wants us to glorify Him in return. He wants to hear us sing, "To God be the glory, great things He hath done!" He desires our praise and thanks. God answers prayer so that we will tell others of His goodness. He desires for you to tell someone about His blessings in your life! He wants us to share the victories with others and glorify Him before men. Friend, if you've been healed, blessed, or cared for, tell someone. If your marriage has been spared by God's grace, tell someone. If someone recognizes God's blessings in your life, don't take the credit. Give God the glory! Allow Him to be manifested as you abide in prayer.

An abiding Christian is a praying Christian. Prayer is what began your relationship with Christ at the moment of your salvation, and prayer is the key to maintaining an abiding relationship with Jesus Christ. Abide with Christ in prayer. Come to Him moment by moment and seek His help in every aspect of your life. He is waiting to meet with you even now.

CHAPTER FIVE

Abiding in His Precepts

Today, there is a war over the Word of God. There is, in a very real sense, a battle for the Bible. There are those who despise it, deny it, and distort it. There are those who love it, believe it, and obey it. To those who obey its commandments, it brings freedom. For those who reject its precepts, it brings oppression. Any nation that violates the Word of God will never prosper.

The Bible says in Proverbs 14:34, *"Righteousness exalteth a nation: but sin is a reproach to any people."* When a nation turns away from the Bible, there will be sorrow, violence, and anarchy in their land.

I thank God for the rich, scriptural heritage of America. Patrick Henry once said, "It cannot be stated too strongly or too loudly that America was founded by Christians with faith in Jesus Christ." John Quincy Adams stated, "The highest glory of the

American Revolution is that we joined together government with the principles of New Testament Christianity."

America was founded upon the principles of the Word of God. The Bible has brought prosperity, joy, and happiness to our shores. Sadly, the more God's Word is removed from the fabric of American culture, the less we will see the blessings of God. No country can prosper when she neglects the teachings of the Word of God. No family can experience joy when they neglect the principles of the Bible. When a marriage fails to love the teachings of Jesus Christ, it will fail in love for one another.

I like what God told Joshua in Joshua 1:8, *"This book of the law shall not depart out of thy mouth; but thou shalt meditate therein day and night, that thou mayest observe to do according to all that is written therein: for then thou shalt make thy way prosperous, and then thou shalt have good success."* When God's man obeys God's Word, he will find liberty, prosperity, and joy in the Christian life. When he chooses to disobey God's Word, he will return to the same bondage from which he was saved. When we abide in His precepts, there is an inner joy that springs up simply because we are obedient to our Maker.

There are three specific products that come into the life of someone who abides in the precepts of Jesus Christ.

Abiding in His Precepts Proves Our Love

Jesus said in John 14:15, *"If ye love me, keep my commandments."* Jesus' message was simple: "If you love Me, demonstrate it by keeping My commandments." No one should ever have to coerce you into serving God or into obeying God. These actions should flow naturally from a heart that loves Jesus Christ and understands His commands.

Jesus elaborates His message in John 14:23–24, *"…If a man love me, he will keep my words: and my Father will love him, and we will come unto him, and make our abode with him. He that loveth me not keepeth not my sayings....*" When we are obedient to the precepts of Jesus Christ, we are proving our love for Him.

There were many commandments Jesus gave His disciples, and there are many commandments He gives to us. One of the very first commandments for a Christian is the command to be baptized. Immediately after baptism, we are commanded to learn the precepts Jesus taught His disciples. Jesus said in Matthew 28:19–20, "*Go ye therefore, and teach all nations, baptizing them in the name of the Father, and of the Son, and of the Holy Ghost: Teaching them to observe all things whatsoever I have commanded you....*"

The final words of Jesus to His disciples were very clear: "Teach others to observe the precepts I have commanded you." As believers, we are disciples of Christ. Therefore, the message is directed to us. Not only are we to obey the teachings of Jesus, but we are to disciple fellow Christians to do the same.

No other man in the Bible could illustrate this truth better than the Apostle Peter. In John 21:15–17, Jesus asks Peter a question that could be asked of us: "*So when they had dined, Jesus saith to Simon Peter, Simon, son of Jonas, lovest thou me more than these? He saith unto him, Yea, Lord; thou knowest that I love thee. He saith unto him, Feed my lambs. He saith to him again the second time, Simon, son of Jonas, lovest thou me? He saith unto him, Yea, Lord; thou knowest that I love thee. He saith unto him, Feed my sheep. He saith unto him the third time, Simon, son of Jonas, lovest thou me? Peter was grieved because he said unto him the third time, Lovest thou me? And he said unto him, Lord, thou knowest all things; thou knowest that I love thee. Jesus saith unto him, Feed my sheep.*"

Peter was much like the average Christian today. He loved the Lord with a brotherly love—he was fond of the Lord. Many people are "fond" of the Lord and His church, but Jesus was not referring to this type of love. He wanted to know if Peter loved

Him with a godly love—a deep, spiritual love that would cause him to forsake this world and serve the Lord. Do you love the Lord with that kind of a love? If you do, you will have no objection to serving the Lord with your whole heart.

Many who sit in church, participate in the services, and claim to love the Lord, never seek to obey His commands. Jesus said in Luke 6:46, *"And why call ye me, Lord, Lord, and do not the things which I say?"* If I *say* I love my wife, but never attend to her requests—I fall short in my love. Why is it that we are quick to accept God's graciousness and forgiveness, but we are slow to accept His commandments? Everyone loves the promises of God, but an abiding Christian will choose to love His precepts as well.

Abiding in His Precepts Provides Assurance in Our Hearts

Assurance in His Love

There is always an assurance that comes into the heart of someone who is obeying the Lord. Jesus said in John 15:10, *"If ye keep my commandments, ye shall abide in my love...."* Each act of obedience on my part will deepen my assurance of His love. On the contrary, each time I disobey the Lord, I am numbing my conscience toward Him and increasing my doubts and uncertainty.

I have never met a Christian who doubted their salvation, who prior to their doubt was not involved in some sort of sin. Jesus was clear— "If you keep my commandments, you will abide in my love. You will not doubt my love. You can strengthen your relationship with Me as you abide day by day in my precepts."

The reason a man may not "feel" saved is because he is not abiding in the commandments of God. Disobedience compounds doubt, but obedience brings a blessed assurance. The more you abide in God's love, the more assurance you will have. As you surrender to Him and obey His commands, you can rest in knowing that you are His!

Assurance Builds Maturity

Assurance provides a basis for spiritual growth. An immature Christian lives a very unstable life. One day he is confident of his salvation; the next day he is unsure. One day he loves the church; the next day he disdains it. One day he keeps the Lord's commandments; the next day he disobeys them. His life could be characterized as a yo-yo. He is up and down—never finding spiritual rest.

People who consistently obey the commandments of the Lord will build maturity and stability. They hear a message; they apply the message. They read the Bible; they apply the Bible. They are consistently obeying the Word of God. Over time they will feel more assured of their relationship with the Lord because they are learning what it means to abide with Christ. Assurance builds itself into maturity. The yo-yo Christian will never mature, but the Christian who abides in the Lord will grow spiritually mature.

Jesus talked about this in 1 John 2:5, *"But whoso keepeth his word, in him verily is the love of God perfected...."* As we continually abide in His precepts, maturity begins to bloom. We are perfected by His precepts.

The psalmist said, *"Thy word have I hid in mine heart...."* Why—just so he can have assurance in his heart? No. *"Thy word have I hid in mine heart that I might not sin against thee."* This could be the testimony of a Christian whose maturity is starting to show forth. He has the assurance of the Word in his heart that is developing maturity and bearing fruit outwardly.

The Apostle Paul said to Timothy in 2 Timothy 2:15, *"Study to shew thyself approved unto God...."* Why? Just so he can have knowledge of the Scriptures? No. *"Study to shew thyself approved unto God, a workman that needeth not to be ashamed...."* God wants His Word to dwell in your heart so that you might have assurance; so that you can be a workman for Him in His vineyard; so that you can bear fruit in the Christian life.

Scott O'Grady survived a life and death ordeal that made headlines and inspired millions. His tale of courage, faith, and quick thinking provides a boost to individuals and organizations facing overwhelming odds. As an Air Force fighter pilot, Captain O'Grady was shot down over Bosnia in 1995, while aiding in the enforcement of the NATO no-fly zone in an F-16. Alone—facing death, capture, and the elements—he discovered within himself the spirit to persevere. He relied on the skills learned during a lifetime of preparing for the unthinkable. Even isolated behind enemy lines, Captain O'Grady remained a member of a carefully drilled team. For six days, insects, grass, and rainwater helped keep him alive in hostile territory. His rescue was contingent on his ability to follow the basic instructions he had been taught.

In the midst of that terrible ordeal, he simply obeyed what he had been taught. He followed the precepts given to him, and that obedience led to his ultimate rescue! We all will experience times in our lives when we are shot down, spiritually speaking. Our best-laid plans will explode, and we will find ourselves behind enemy lines fighting for our lives. Knowing, remembering, and obeying God's precepts will bring security and safety during these times.

It is only when we abide in God's precepts that we can have the assurance necessary to prevail. When we apply the precepts we have learned in "basic training," rescue will be on the way.

Abiding in His Precepts Promotes a Loving Spirit

Finally, abiding in the precepts of the Word of God will cause my love for God and others to grow. Jesus said in John 15:12, *"This is my commandment, That ye love one another, as I have loved you."*

When we obey the commandments of the Lord, we love others the way Jesus would love them. In John 13:34 Jesus said, *"A new commandment I give unto you, That ye love one another; as I have loved you, that ye also love one another."*

If we abide in the precepts of the Word of God we will encourage a loving spirit back into our family, our church, and our workplace. We will rekindle the fire in our marriage.

Love is not a syrupy emotion. Love is the act of your will to obey God. It is a decision of your will to do what is right. God commands us to *"love one another."* As you abide in His Word—His precepts—you will discover that God's truth will produce a loving spirit within you. Others will notice! You will make a difference as God's love springs out from within.

There is too much surface Christianity today. There are many who talk the talk, but do not walk the walk. Jesus sees your heart, and others need to see God's love and presence in you.

Abiding in Christ involves more than feeling warm and fuzzy about Him. Abiding in Him involves abiding in His Word with a heart to obey His commands. As you read His Word and follow His commands, you will prove your love to Him, build maturity in your life, and exhibit a loving spirit to those around you. Allow God's Word to change your life. Choose to abide in His precepts today!

CHAPTER SIX

Abiding in His Pleasure

When Harry Truman became president, he worried about losing touch with common, everyday Americans, so he would often go out and spend time among them.

One evening, Truman decided to stroll down to the Memorial Bridge on the Potomac River. While there, he became curious about the mechanism that raised and lowered the middle span of the bridge. He made his way across the catwalks and through the inner workings of the bridge, and suddenly he came upon the bridge tender, eating his evening supper out of a tin bucket.

The man showed absolutely no surprise when he looked up and saw the best-known and most powerful man in the world. He just swallowed his food, wiped his mouth, smiled, and said, "You know, Mr. President, I was just thinking of you."

It was a greeting that Truman adored and never forgot.

Wouldn't it be wonderful, when Jesus Christ suddenly appears in the clouds, if we could say, "You know, Lord, I was just thinking of You." You can, if you will discover the great pleasure and joy of abiding in Christ.

There is no doubt the message of Jesus was on the hearts and minds of His disciples as they made their way to the Garden of Gethsemane. Our Lord had just shared a sobering message. In John 14, He told them of His soon departure, yet assured them of His future return. He also promised to send them a "Comforter"—the Holy Spirit. While the thought of a Comforter was wonderful, I am sure in the minds of the disciples, it was difficult to comprehend exactly how this "Comforter" would be real to them.

In John 15, Jesus again turned to His disciples and told them of His desire that they abide in Him and bear much fruit. All that Jesus shared in these two chapters was very serious in nature when you consider that the disciples were relatively new Christians. Jesus was preparing them for His journey to Calvary. He shared His burden. I can almost sense the responsibility the disciples must have felt as Jesus communicated His soon-coming death.

Jesus said in John 15:11, *"These things have I spoken unto you, that my joy might remain in you, and that your joy might be full."* Jesus indicated to His disciples that everything He had been telling them, though serious in nature, was so that their joy would be full. Jesus wanted them to have abundant joy.

The Christian who abides in Jesus Christ will abide in His pleasure and will know the joy of the Lord. Christianity will not be a "duty" but a "delight." This is what Jesus wants for you. Yes, He gives us a Bible full of commandments, but not so that our lives will be drudgery. Jesus gives us these commandments so that we can experience true joy.

The Conditions for Joy

The Bible says in verse 11, *"These things have I spoken unto you...."* To have joy as God's child, you must listen to the Word of God.

Jesus speaks words of joy in this passage that He expects us to hear and receive. If we do not listen to the words of our Lord, we cannot experience true joy in the Christian life.

Charles Spurgeon, the great English preacher of last century, said his objective was not only that we would know the truth, but that we would have joy in the truth. Jesus does not want us to come to church to gather truth intellectually. He wants us to have joy in our hearts because of the truths learned. This is what Jesus meant when He said, *"And ye shall know the truth, and the truth shall make you free"* (John 8:32). The truth of the Word of God brings freedom and joy into the heart of a Christian.

I have no doubt that God speaks to us through His Word. The question is not, "Is God still speaking to men?" The question is, "Are we listening to God?" Jesus is speaking—are you listening? Sometimes, we listen to everything but the words of Jesus.

The world is speaking to us through media. People are speaking to us through personal experience. To whom will you listen? If you are depending on people or circumstances for your joy, then you have not learned the truth of abiding in His pleasure. Abiding in His pleasure begins when we listen to the words of Jesus. We need Jesus twenty-four hours a day, seven days a week.

Hear the Word of God

The conditions for joy begin with hearing, believing, and obeying the words of Christ. I must act upon what Jesus is saying. I must apply what Jesus is teaching. The question is not, "Do you believe Philippians 4:4 when it says, *'Rejoice in the Lord alway: and again I say, Rejoice'*?" The real question is, "Will you rejoice in the Lord?"

Respond to the Word of God

God is sovereign. He knows every decision we are going to make before we ever make it. But, realize God has given to us a *free will.*

We choose whether or not we want joy when we choose to listen to His words.

God's Word is clear. I must make the decision to respond to the Word of God. Habakkuk said in Habakkuk 3:17–18, *"Although the fig tree shall not blossom, neither shall fruit be in the vines; the labour of the olive shall fail, and the fields shall yield no meat; the flock shall be cut off from the fold, and there shall be no herd in the stalls: Yet I will rejoice in the LORD, I will joy in the God of my salvation."* Habakkuk said, "I don't care what I lose. I don't care if I lose all of my money, my flocks, and my crops. I still am determined to rejoice in God and in the joy of my salvation."

The word *joy* is mentioned nineteen times in the book of Philippians. Happiness is a choice. You cannot depend upon your circumstances, your job, your health, your family, your friends, or even your church to find joy. You must decide now that you are going to find it in the Word of God that never changes. The conditions for joy are quite simple—hear God's Word, believe it, and obey it. It's your choice.

The Constancy of Joy

Philippians 2:5 says, *"Let this mind be in you, which was also in Christ Jesus."* As long as I have the mind of Christ through the Word of God, there will be joy in my life. As long as I am abiding in the Lord daily, all fear fades away.

His Joy Remains as We Focus on His Word

The Bible says in James 1:8, *"A double minded man is unstable in all his ways."* Christians struggle with consistent joy due to double mindedness and a lack of stability. We're up one day and down the next—like a roller coaster. Our highs and lows are varied. Rather than anchoring our hearts to truth and letting God's Word give us stability, we let our emotions dictate our attitude toward spiritual things.

His Joy Prevails over Any Heartache

Most of my relatives live in Colorado. My grandfather was a man who loved his family, his church, and farming. In the particular community where he lived, several of the farmhouses did not have county water supply, so trucks often brought in a sufficient supply of water.

Often, my cousin and I would drive a water truck to get water, then we would empty the tank into the well at the farm.

One day, we jumped into the cab and took off to fill up the truck. On the way there we stopped at a gas station to refuel the truck and to grab something to eat. When we finally reached our destination, we backed up the truck, connected the water hose to the top of the truck, and released the valve.

We were set. We walked around to the front of the truck, sat on the bumper and pulled out our Snickers bars and Dr. Peppers. This was the life! It was a gorgeous day. The weather was perfect, and the Rocky Mountains before us never looked more beautiful.

Several minutes had passed when I noticed a pool of water forming around my feet. I jumped up, turned around, and saw a pond engulfing our truck. Somehow, we had not been careful to attach the lines correctly and now water was going everywhere except in the tank. Hundreds of gallons of water had missed the tank. The water was free. All we had to do was align the truck. But instead, hundreds of gallons of water was wasted.

The reason many Christians never experience joy is not because Jesus has a supply shortage. He has all the joy you could ever want, and the best part is—it's free! The problem is that we forget to align ourselves with His Word. There are times we need to pull up and say, "Lord, if there is any sin blocking Your joy—

remove it. I want my tank to be in perfect alignment to receive water. I want my life to be in a position to receive Your joy."

Jesus said, "...*that my joy might remain in you.*" His joy can prevail over any heartache on this earth, because His joy is based upon His resurrection.

The greatest illustration of this truth is found in Hebrews 12:2, "*Looking unto Jesus the author and finisher of our faith; who for the joy that was set before him endured the cross, despising the shame, and is set down at the right hand of the throne of God.*" While hanging on the Cross, Jesus suffered the most excruciating pain any man has ever suffered.

The Bible tells us He despised the shame. He was able to endure the Cross. How? He looked forward to the joy set before Him. Jesus Christ focused on the empty tomb. He focused on sitting on the right hand of God the Heavenly Father. He focused on the millions of people who would have their sins forgiven and would spend eternity with Him in Heaven. "...*For the joy that was set before him endured the cross....*"

Let the joy of the Bible sink into your heart. It does not matter what trial you are experiencing. It does not matter what burden you are bearing. Joy has been set before you, and you can endure. (By the way, it is not a temporary joy. It is an everlasting joy!)

Maybe your teenager is following a path you fear. Maybe your home has been splintered. Maybe there is ice in the pit of your stomach every time you open the mailbox for fear of another bill you cannot pay. No matter your situation, no matter your cross—there is joy for you.

The psalmist said in Psalm 30:5, "...*weeping may endure for a night, but joy cometh in the morning.*" You may be experiencing the darkest night of your life. Your strength may be faint and your hope may be dim, but hold on! The dawn is coming. For with each new day brings a new beginning. His joy is always available.

The Completeness of His Joy

Jesus concludes John 15:11 with this exciting statement: *"These things have I spoken unto you, that my joy might remain in you, and that your joy might be full."* Our Lord gives us an undeniable promise—not only can our joy remain constant, but it can be full.

Everyone wants to be full. You never want to leave a restaurant or a gas station half empty. It is the same with the Christian life; Jesus intends for our lives to be full of joy. Jesus wants you to be so filled with His joy that when the devil brings his plate of temptation your way, you can say emphatically, "No way! I am so full of the love of God and the teachings of His Word, I cannot accept." That is what the Bible means when it says, *"…for the joy of the LORD is your strength"* (Nehemiah 8:10).

The pleasure of an abiding relationship with Christ is unlike anything this world has to offer. The world offers amusement parks and ball games that give us temporary satisfaction. But, when the fun is over, only a feeling of emptiness remains. Jesus promises that, even when the "fun" is over, we can still have joy. In Psalm 16:11 the psalmist said, *"…in thy presence is fullness of joy…."* When we are in the presence of the Lord, gathered around His Word, there is fullness of joy.

Are you happy in the Lord? Is the joy of the Lord your strength? Have you been sitting at Satan's dining table? If you are filled with the world's cares and philosophies, you cannot be filled with the joy of the Lord. Is the Christian life a pleasure to you? If you are not experiencing joy, you are not abiding in Christ. But, when you are abiding in Him, remaining in Him, and living out His Word, you can experience full and abundant joy.

When Jesus invites us to abide in Him, He invites us into a relationship of delight, not a system of duty. Simply put, an abiding Christian is a joyful Christian. Jesus intends that our daily walk with Him would bring great pleasure and rejoicing into our lives, in spite of life's hardships and unpredictable circumstances.

The happiness of the world is fleeting and temporary, but the joy of Jesus Christ is abundant and eternal. He desires to fill you with His joy if you will abide in Him, abide in His Word, and obey His commands.

Abiding in Christ and obeying His Word are the only certain paths to true joy. As you hear and respond to the Word of God, you will find the constant, complete joy for which your heart is longing!

CHAPTER SEVEN

Abiding in His Provision

John 15:12 says, *"This is my commandment, That ye love one another, as I have loved you."* Take a moment to think about God's love. Now, make it personal—"God loves *me*!" What an incredible truth that God knows me, yet He still loves me! The Author of the Bible, the Creator of the universe, and the Saviour of the world loves me, cares for me, and longs to abide with me.

I have had many days in my life that were less than good. I have experienced heartache, disappointment, and regret, but the one truth that sustains me is God's love. He loves me—individually! God's love is more than just a bumper sticker statement. It is a reality.

One of the qualifying characteristics of Christ's love is "giving." Jesus didn't just talk about love, He showed His love in John 15:13, *"Greater love hath no man than this, that a man lay down his life for his friends."*

Amy Carmichael, a missionary to India for fifty-six years, made this statement: "You can give without loving, but you cannot love without giving." Jesus expressed His love by giving. True Christian love always expresses itself in giving. True love involves an act of my will to meet the needs of another.

If a husband says to his wife, "I love you," he must also express that love by acting in his own will to meet his wife's needs. When he fails to give, he fails to provide her with true love.

In the same way, when God expresses His love toward us, He does so by giving. He goes beyond the words—He provides. Let's take a closer look at the incredible provision of the love of God in our lives.

God's Love Provides a Pardon

All Men Deserve Judgment

Again, John 15:13 shows us, *"Greater love hath no man than this, that a man lay down his life for his friends."* To understand the significance of Jesus Christ dying on the Cross, we must first realize all men deserve judgment.

People often wonder why Jesus Christ died. To understand the answer, you have to remember a man named Adam. God created Adam and Eve as sinless human beings, and they fellowshipped with God in the Garden of Eden. They lived in a perfect creation—no crime, no pain, no injustice, and no disease. But one day Adam and Eve made a terrible choice. God gave them freedom to eat of any tree in the garden except the Tree of the Knowledge of Good and Evil. After the commandment was given, the serpent beguiled Eve, and she and her husband ate of the fruit of the tree.

As soon as they had partaken of the fruit, the Bible says, They transgressed against God. That evening, when God came to commune with them, they were hiding from Him. As a result of their sin, God banished them from the Garden of Eden. Since that day, every human born into this world has been born a sinner in need of a Saviour. Romans 5:12 sums it up when it says, *"Wherefore, as by one man sin entered into the world, and death by sin; and so death passed upon all men, for that all have sinned."*

My wife and I have four children, and each one is unique. We have never taught them "how" to sin. It came very naturally. In fact, if you are ever dealing with someone who denies inherent sin, invite him to a tour of your church nursery. He will soon discover that children are not satisfied with their one toy. They will kick, scream, hit, shove, and sometimes bite until they can have the other child's toy. Who taught them that? No one. Sin comes naturally to every human.

All men are born in a sinful condition, which means that all men are condemned before God. The Bible speaks of this in Romans 3:23, *"For all have sinned…."* Romans 6:23 says, *"For the wages of sin is death; but the gift of God is eternal life through Jesus Christ our Lord."* The payment for sin is death. All men deserve judgment.

Christ's Sacrifice Provides a Pardon

Some people hear of Christ's death, and it has no significance or meaning. This is because they have never made it personal. Jesus laid down His life to pardon the world from sin and future judgment—that sounds very broad. Jesus gave His life to pardon me from my sins and give me a home in Heaven—this gives Calvary much more significance on a personal level.

The Bible relates the significance of Christ's pardon in James 5:20, *"Let him know, that he which converteth the sinner from the error of his way shall save a soul from death…."* God's Word teaches the difference between a physical death and a spiritual death. Without Jesus Christ, a man must die physically *and* spiritually. With Christ, a man who dies physically can escape spiritual death and have eternal life with God.

A person will never appreciate God's *pardon* unless he understands the *penalty*. God's Word says in Romans 5:10–11, *"For if, when we were enemies, we were reconciled to God by the death of his Son, much more, being reconciled, we shall be saved by his life. And not only so, but we also joy in God through our Lord Jesus Christ, by whom we have now received the atonement."*

All of us were dead in sins, guilty, and deserving of judgment. There was only one hope—atonement! Someone had to pay for our sin. The only One worthy of paying for our sin was Someone who had no sin of His own. Yet, there was no man good enough to pay for the sins of men, because all men are sinners. So Jesus Christ, Who had no sin, came and provided atonement for every sinner who will accept His payment. Jesus' death was a substitutionary death. He took our penalty so that we could be set free.

Isaiah referred to this in Isaiah 53:5, *"But he was wounded for our transgressions, he was bruised for our iniquities: the chastisement of our peace was upon him; and with his stripes we are healed."* Jesus died for you and me that we might be "pardoned" from our sin.

Growing up in Sunday school, I would sing, "What can wash away my sin?" And the answer would come back resoundingly, "Nothing but the blood of Jesus." No church can forgive sins. No baptistry water can wash away sins. Only the blood of Jesus Christ can pardon sin.

God's Love Provides Partnership

We Are Friends of the King

The Bible says in John 15:14–15, *"Ye are my friends, if ye do whatsoever I command you. Henceforth I call you not servants; for the servant knoweth not what his lord doeth: but I have called you friends...."* The word *friend* in this passage means "friend in the court" or "friend in the inner circle." When I trusted Jesus Christ as my personal Saviour, I became a "friend of the King."

Friends of a king are close to him, but they still obey him. You can be a friend and a servant at the same time. Nehemiah was the cupbearer for King Artaxerxes during the captivity period of the Jewish people. He was a "friend" of the king, but he was also a "servant" of the king. The Bible says Abraham was a "friend of God," but he was also the "servant of God." King David had many mighty men around him who were his friends, but the desire of those friends was to meet the king's needs.

What kind of friend are you to Jesus? Are you an abiding friend? Are you a serving friend? Are you an obedient friend?

Jesus calls those who are saved *His* friends. True friends delight in serving. What is Jesus asking you to do that seems too sacrificial? Whatever it may be, it could never be compared to the price He paid when He died upon the Cross.

We Are Servants of the King

When I was a junior-aged boy, I had a friend in church whose uncle was Hall of Fame Brooks Robinson—a famous baseball player for the Baltimore Orioles. One evening, he arranged for us to see Brooks Robinson play. We even had special passes to see him and the team before they played.

We felt significant as we strutted around the locker room looking for Brooks Robinson. Finally, we met him. If I had a brain, I would have taken some baseball cards and had them signed. But I didn't. All I did was stand there and marvel! Here I was meeting this famous baseball player in person. He was so glad to see his nephew, my friend, and he greeted me and treated me so well. Later, we all had pictures taken with him by the team photographer. I felt like a real "somebody" that day.

If Brooks Robinson would have said to me, "Hey, son, I need a glass of water." I would have said, "Yes, sir!" and would have run to retrieve it. If he would have said, "Clean my cleats." I would have responded, "Sure, I'll clean your cleats." There is not a thing he could have asked me to do that I would not have delighted in doing.

If I am on the "inner court" of Jesus Christ, my delight should be in serving Him. Why is it when Jesus asks us to serve Him, we respond with hesitation—when He asks us to witness to our friend or co-worker, we decline? "Lord, I know I am Your friend, but I am busy. I have things to do. I don't clean cleats. I am just not one to run and get water. I am embarrassed when I do that."

Are you His friend?

God's Love Provides a Perspective on Service

The Bible says in John 15:15–16, "*Henceforth I call you not servants; for the servant knoweth not what his lord doeth: but I have called you friends; for all things that I have heard of my Father I have made known unto you. Ye have not chosen me, but I have chosen you, and ordained you, that ye should go and bring forth fruit, and that your fruit should remain....*"

Since we are friends of Jesus Christ, He allows us to understand the "big picture" of His purpose for our lives. He gives us a new perspective on life! Jesus said in John 15:15, "*...for all things that I have heard of my Father I have made known unto you.*" A servant sees only the small part of the wall he is building, but a friend knows what the whole building is going to look like. Jesus assures us that we are not just servants doing a job. We are friends sharing in the vision.

The Holy Spirit Guides Us

God allows the Holy Spirit to guide us in understanding the Word of God. John 16:12–13 says, "*I have yet many things to say unto you, but ye cannot bear them now. Howbeit when he, the Spirit of truth, is come, he will guide you into all truth....*" How can I understand the Bible? How can I comprehend God's perspective on life? The Holy Spirit guides us in an understanding of these things, and He helps us understand and follow God's true purpose for our lives.

The Lord Has Chosen Us for a Purpose

Jesus said in John 15:16, *"Ye have not chosen me, but I have chosen you, and ordained you, that ye should go and bring forth fruit...."* The word *chosen* means "chosen for a purpose." It does not mean that Jesus was destining some people to Heaven and some people to Hell. Second Peter 3:9 dispels this myth when it conveys God is *"...not willing that any should perish, but that all should come to repentance."* Revelation 22:17 extends the invitation to anyone who wants to be saved when it says, *"...And whosoever will, let him take the water of life freely."*

Friend, God has a purpose for your life, and He will reveal that purpose to you as you abide in Him. He has chosen you! He has *"ordained you."* The word *ordained* means "placed in ministry." Whether or not you feel that you've been called into ministry, *every* child of God has been placed into the ministry. Perhaps you thought that only preachers were ordained, but every *saint* is called to be a *servant.* Jesus desires that every Christian would serve Him in ministry. Why? The answer is found in John 15:16, *"...that ye should go and bring forth fruit, and that your fruit should remain...."* God's plan for ordaining us is so that we might bear spiritual fruit.

Several years ago, I visited a member in our church who was having serious health problems. He was ninety-three years old. One afternoon he said to me, "Pastor, I just wish the Lord would take me home. I'm just ready to go to Heaven." A picture of his wife was there on the wall behind him. I knew he missed her. It was obvious he was ready to meet her again.

I assured him that the Lord still had a purpose for him to fulfill. As long as he had breath—God had a plan. "God does not work by accident," I told him.

He cried for a moment. Then he said, "I know…I know… God has a purpose for me. I know there is something left for me to do. I know that is why God has me here." Not long ago, God allowed that man to fulfill his purpose. He is now reunited with his wife.

Some time ago, a San Jose, California newspaper headline caught my attention. It said, "One Thousandth Person Jumps from Golden Gate Bridge." I was struck that in a city flaunting civil rights and perversion, one thousand people had jumped off a bridge into eternity. What a powerful reminder that sin never satisfies.

There are three primary reasons that people consider suicide. First, they feel as though "no one loves them." Second, they feel they have "no true friends." Third, they believe they have "no real purpose in life—no reason to go on living."

Amazingly, the three things our hearts cry for the most, Jesus promises! He answers our needs before we even realize what they are! He invites us into an abiding relationship with Him where we can find true love, close friendship, and an eternal purpose. What a wonderful provision from a wonderful Saviour!

Harriet Beecher Stowe, in her booklet, *How to Live in Christ*, made this statement: "How does the branch bear fruit? Not by incessant effort for sunshine and air; not by vain struggles—it simply abides in the vine, in silent and undisturbed union, and blossoms, and fruit appear as of spontaneous growth."

As you abide in Christ, a wonderful transformation will happen—you will become like Him. God's ultimate will for every believer is to be conformed to the image of His Son. This leads us to part two of our study. Let's discover how this wonderful abiding relationship will change us to be more like Jesus Christ.

Becoming Like Christ

CHAPTER EIGHT

God's Perspective on Salvation
Romans 8:28–30

The greatest privilege in my life is knowing Jesus Christ as my personal Saviour. I can look back on the day I was saved with joy and gratitude. Although I may not have known everything about God or the Bible, I realized the purpose for my salvation. Primarily, I desired to have my sins forgiven, to know God for all of eternity, and to be set free from the bondage of sin. When I was confronted with the Gospel, I received enough information to make the best decision of my life.

Obviously, your reasons for accepting Christ were very clear. You realized that you were a sinner destined for hell, and that God had provided a way of escape through His Son's death on the Cross. You chose to believe in Him for salvation and to receive His gift of eternal life.

The Purpose of Salvation

In a previous chapter, we discovered that God's purpose for believers is to bear fruit—both the fruit of the Spirit and the fruit of winning souls. Now, let us turn our focus to God's purpose of transformation in our lives.

You know why you asked Jesus Christ to be your Saviour, but have you ever wondered what His long-term plan is for your life? Romans 8:28 says, *"And we know that all things work together for good to them that love God, to them who are the called according to his purpose."* As we grow toward spiritual maturity, we will stop focusing on what we received out of salvation, and we will turn our attention toward how we can fulfill God's purpose for our future.

> *For whom he did foreknow, he also did predestinate to be conformed to the image of his Son, that he might be the firstborn among many brethren.*—ROMANS 8:29

To Be Conformed to the Image of Christ

You were redeemed unto God so His will could be accomplished through your life. You must remember it is God who called you, and it is God who accomplishes His will in your life.

We will never become perfect like Jesus Christ, spiritually or physically, until we see Him face to face. It is His will however, that we grow in His Word and conform to the image of His Son while we are living on earth. God, according to His divine omnipotence, has promised to complete the work He has begun in our lives. God's plan for believers was predetermined. You can rest in God's promise of eternal life and focus on His purpose of conforming your life to the image of Jesus Christ.

In Heaven, God will sanctify us in the image of Christ, we will experience spiritual conformity to Him, and we will be completely set apart by the will of God. Our sin nature will no longer hinder us, and we will live in perfect obedience and compliance to God's righteousness.

We will be like Him! First John 3:2 says, *"Beloved, now are we the sons of God, and it doth not yet appear what we shall be: but we know that, when he shall appear, we shall be like him; for we shall see him as he is."*

When we see Jesus, we will be in His likeness, and we will have a resurrected body that feels no pain or sickness. The trials that we endure on this earth will seem small to us in eternity. The cancer that plagues many and the physical limitations of others will be changed into a glorified body for all of eternity. We will be completely whole—physically and spiritually.

A little girl asked her grandpa, "Did God make you?" "He sure did," was the reply. For several minutes she studied her grandpa's features, and then she caught a glimpse of herself in the mirror. At last she said, "You know, Grandpa, God is doing a much better job lately." One day, we will all have glorified bodies! But until then, God desires to conform us into His image.

To Make Christ Preeminent

God did not save you to bring glory to yourself; He saved you so that He could be praised and magnified. Romans 8:29 says, *"For whom he did foreknow, he also did predestinate to be conformed to the image of his Son, that he might be the firstborn among many brethren."* God wants you to become like Him, and by doing so, recognize that He is the firstborn among many brethren. The term *firstborn* was used in Jewish culture to speak about preeminence or to depict a privileged status. God is perfect in His attributes and sacrificial in His love. He deserves the preeminence in our lives.

> *And he is the head of the body, the church: who is the beginning, the firstborn from the dead; that in all things he might have the preeminence.*—COLOSSIANS 1:18

Someday soon, we will gather around Jesus Christ in Heaven. We will sing His praise; He will have the preeminence; and we will finally understand God's fulfilled purpose in conforming us to Christ's image. We will no longer experience the heartache of sin or the pain of sickness. For the first time, we will be completely like Jesus Christ. And, He will be high and lifted up on His heavenly throne.

The Plan of Salvation

Your Predetermined Destiny

God's plan for salvation was based on His foreknowledge in eternity past. Verse 29 says, *"For whom he did foreknow, he also did predestinate...."* The word *foreknowledge* is based on the Greek word *proginosko* which means "to know ahead." The Bible says that God is omniscient, or all-knowing. In His providence, He sees all things ahead of time.

No one can fathom the omniscience of God or comprehend His knowledge; therefore, God provided a plan of salvation for all people. He saw down through the ages, and predetermined everlasting life in Heaven for those who would accept His Son. God beheld your faith in advance of your life. Jeremiah 1:5 states, *"Before I formed thee in the belly I knew thee...."* It is humbling to recognize that God loved you and provided you with a plan of redemption even before your birth. He knew every sin you would commit and all of your shortcomings and failures, yet He still loved you.

> *In whom also we have obtained an inheritance, being predestinated according to the purpose of him who worketh all things after the counsel of his own will.*
> —EPHESIANS 1:11

The word *predestination* deals with God predetermining you to conform to His image. In other words, God already knows your destiny. He wants you to live for Him and to become conformed to the image of His Son.

Because your destiny was predetermined, you can have the assurance that all things work together for good. There are no mistakes with God. As you understand this doctrine, you will not question God's goodness during times of trials. You will not turn back on your faith when adversity comes into your life.

A Call to His Destiny

God not only predetermines your destiny, He calls you to fulfill His will. He desires that you would accept Him as your Saviour and conform your life to the image of His Son. Romans 8:30 says, *"Moreover whom he did predestinate, them he also called: and whom he called, them he also justified: and whom he justified, them he also glorified."*

The first step to fulfilling God's will is to accept His gift of eternal life. When you feel conviction to repent of your sins, God's Spirit touches your heart and calls you to salvation. Second Timothy 1:9 states, *"Who hath saved us, and called us with an holy calling, not according to our works, but according to his own purpose and grace, which was given us in Christ Jesus before the world began."*

While it is comforting to know that God has a predetermined plan for your life, what good will that plan accomplish if He has not also called you to fulfill it? The fact that He "calls" indicates that you must answer. You must exercise your will. Sometimes it is hard to comprehend the balancing point between God's predetermined will and man's free will. Yet, we simply need to understand this side of Heaven that God is calling us, and we have a responsibility to respond to His call. God predetermined your destiny and called you to His destiny, and He also paid for your destiny by shedding His blood for your sin.

He that believeth on him is not condemned: but he that believeth not is condemned already, because he hath not believed in the name of the only begotten Son of God.—JOHN 3:18

I believe that God has given man a choice—*"that whosoever will may come."* He does not limit atonement; man limits atonement by rejecting God. Second Peter 3:9 reminds us, *"The Lord is not slack concerning his promise, as some men count slackness; but is longsuffering to us-ward, not willing that any should perish, but that all should come to repentance."*

Being justified freely by his grace through the redemption that is in Christ Jesus: Whom God hath set forth to be a propitiation through faith in his blood, to declare his righteousness for the remission of sins that are past, through the forbearance of God.—ROMANS 3:24–25

Balancing a checkbook can be one of the most frustrating things in life. Sometimes it may take me several hours to justify my bank statement with the figures in my checkbook. As difficult as this can be at times, once my account is made right, there is a sense of accomplishment and security.

Spiritual justification refers to someone being made right with God. You were justified—declared righteous—the day you accepted Christ as your Saviour. God saw your sin, and He said, "That's not right." Therefore, He sacrificed His Son on the Cross in complete payment for your salvation. Your spiritual account was not only made right, it was settled for all of eternity on that day.

God's perspective is not limited; He sees from the beginning to the end. Those of us who have been justified are a glorified people in God's eyes. Our position is already secure in Heaven. God says, "It is done." Second Corinthians 4:17–18 reaffirms this thought, *"For our light affliction, which is but for a moment, worketh for us a far more exceeding and eternal weight of glory; While we look not at the things which are seen, but at the things which are not seen: for the things which are seen are temporal; but the things which are not seen are eternal.*" When God speaks of our glorification, He is referring to our eternal state as His children. How wonderful it is to know that our destiny is settled forever with our Saviour!

The Priority of Sanctification

God's purpose for you and me is to conform to His image—to become more like Jesus Christ. This thought leads me to ask, "Does God want my life to reflect Him now, or is this something that takes place only when I reach Heaven? Am I to respond to trials and difficult circumstances like the rest of the world, or does God have an ongoing growth process for my life now?"

> *But ye are not in the flesh, but in the Spirit, if so be that the Spirit of God dwell in you. Now if any man have not the Spirit of Christ, he is none of his. For as many as are led by the Spirit of God, they are the sons of God. For ye have not received the spirit of bondage again to fear; but ye have received the Spirit of adoption, whereby we cry, Abba, Father.*—ROMANS 8:9,14–15

God is not only interested in our ultimate glorification; He is also interested in our current sanctification. This is the ongoing work of the Spirit, whereby He leads our lives into the likeness of Jesus Christ. The Holy Spirit took residence in our hearts on the day of our salvation, and He now guides us in the process of becoming more like Jesus Christ.

You must realize that becoming like Christ is progressive. You do not automatically become godly the day you accept Jesus as your Saviour. Rules and standards may be necessary at times, but they are not tools of change. For example, some churches may require their ushers to wear a suit coat and tie while serving. Is this requirement a tool for spiritual change? No. Anyone can look sharp on the outside and live an inward life of wickedness and immorality.

As a pastor, I cannot legislate morality. I cannot change someone from the outside, because sin is a matter of the heart. Romans 8:13 says, *"For if ye live after the flesh, ye shall die: but if ye through the Spirit do mortify the deeds of the body, ye shall live."* The Holy Spirit desires to change your life. He wants to do a work in your heart from the inside out. Do you trust God enough to allow Him to work in your heart today?

God has a wonderful purpose in your salvation. He planned from eternity to conform you to the image of Jesus Christ through the process of sanctification. Today, you are either slowly conforming to this world or you are becoming more like Jesus Christ. Which is it?

Paul said in Romans 12:2, *"And be not conformed to this world: but be ye transformed by the renewing of your mind, that ye may prove what is that good, and acceptable, and perfect, will of God."* God's purpose for your salvation is clear—He wants you to become like His Son. As you allow the Holy Spirit and the Word of God to work in your heart, you will experience spiritual sanctification.

> *Till we all come in the unity of the faith, and of the knowledge of the Son of God, unto a perfect man, unto the measure of the stature of the fulness of Christ.*
> —EPHESIANS 4:13

Becoming like Christ begins with understanding God's purpose for saving you. Sure, He desires to give you a home in Heaven, but there's more to it! He desires to change you, grow you, and mature you in His grace. Only God's grace can accomplish the miraculous process that we will study in the coming pages, and as you yield to His power, your life will be different for His glory!

CHAPTER NINE

The Need for Change
Romans 6:1–11

A man from the back mountains of Tennessee took his family to a shopping center in the big city. While there, he had his first encounter with an elevator. He watched as an old, haggardly looking woman hobbled in and the doors closed behind her. A few minutes later, the doors opened, and a young, attractive woman marched smartly off the elevator. The father hollered to his young son, "Billy, go get mother and let's run her through this thing!"

From the beginning of time, God has known you and desired that you would reflect His glory by experiencing a changed life. First Peter 2:9 says, *"But ye are a chosen generation, a royal priesthood, an holy nation, a peculiar people; that ye should shew forth the praises of him who hath called you out of darkness into his marvellous light."*

If you desire to become more like Christ, you first must recognize that God's work of sanctification, which began at the moment of salvation, is an ongoing process. It is the miracle of a moment, but the process of a lifetime. You must recognize your need for a changed life—for spiritual growth. There is nothing more repulsive than a Christian who thinks he has arrived spiritually. You must be willing to say, "I still need to grow in the grace and knowledge of the Lord Jesus Christ." This must be your daily desire for the rest of your life!

I remember when our son, Larry, who is now an adult, was born at the Kaiser Hospital in Santa Clara, California. We were so excited to have a little boy. A few days after his birth, the doctors said that there seemed to be a problem with his blood count. It looked as if he had contracted a virus. As a result, our baby was not gaining weight; he cried constantly; and his temperature was dangerously high. My heart went out to Larry as the doctors pricked, poked, and put him through numerous tests. Day after day, our concerns grew, because there was no growth in his little body.

As tragic as it was when Larry's tiny body would not grow, it is more tragic when someone who claims to know Jesus Christ as his Saviour remains in an anemic condition—a state where there is no change or spiritual growth. God's will is that we would be changing and conforming into the image of His Son on a daily basis.

There are several important truths we must understand if we are going to stand out from the crowd as a "peculiar people" unto Christ.

We Must Agree that We Need Change

To become like Christ, we must realize that we need to change. Notice what Paul says in Romans 6:1, *"What shall we say then? Shall we continue in sin, that grace may abound?"* Paul is asking, "Now that we are saved and forgiven, now that we are under the grace of God, should we just go on living the way we have always lived, or should there be a change?" Paul answers his own question at the end of verse one and in verse two, *"God forbid. How shall we, that are dead to sin, live any longer therein?"* God's grace is not a license to sin—we cannot go about our Christian life by living like the world. God does not intend for us to remain the same after our salvation. His plan is one of radical transformation.

As born-again Christians, change is needful in our lives because of our sinful nature. If we do not recognize that our sinful nature was crucified at the Cross, we will never experience victory. Romans 6:3–4 says, *"Know ye not, that so many of us as were baptized into Jesus Christ were baptized into his death? Therefore we are buried with him by baptism into death: that like as Christ was raised up from the dead by the glory of the Father, even so we also should walk in newness of life."*

These verses are often used to speak of water baptism, but there is also a deeper meaning. When you accepted Christ as your Saviour, you identified with His death, burial, and resurrection. You reckoned the fact that your sins were nailed to the Cross, and that the power of sin was defeated, so that you could walk in newness of life. If you dwell on past sins and failures, God will never be able to use you to your full potential! There must be a change of focus from the old sins to God's purpose for your life.

Romans 6:5–6 says, *"For if we have been planted together in the likeness of his death, we shall be also in the likeness of his resurrection: Knowing this, that our old man is crucified with him, that the body of sin might be destroyed, that henceforth we should not serve sin."* God has provided a victory over the "old man," and it is not normal for a Christian to be bound to that nature—to repeatedly fall into the same patterns of sin. If we truly love the Lord and are seeking to become more like Him, our focus will be so fixed upon Him that we won't want to follow after sin any longer!

A Sunday school teacher was trying to teach this truth to her class one Sunday morning. After her lesson, she said, "Boys and girls, it is now time for the morning worship service. Who can tell me why it is necessary to be quiet in church?" One little girl raised her hand and sweetly replied, "Because people are sleeping." In that statement, the little girl proved that the natural man does not desire the things of God. He wants his fleshly appetites to be appeased. Although our flesh is weak, we must ask the Lord every day to change us into His image and to help us live in victory over the flesh.

> This I say then, Walk in the Spirit, and ye shall not fulfill the lust of the flesh. For the flesh lusteth against the Spirit, and the Spirit against the flesh: and these are contrary the one to the other: so that ye cannot do the things that ye would. But if ye be led of the Spirit, ye are not under the law. Now the works of the flesh are manifest, which are these; Adultery, fornication, uncleanness, lasciviousness, Idolatry, witchcraft, hatred, variance, emulations, wrath, strife, seditions, heresies, Envyings, murders, drunkenness, revellings, and such like: of the which I tell you before, as I have also told you in time past, that they which do such things shall not inherit the kingdom of God.—GALATIANS 5:16–21

The flesh does not always manifest itself in such wicked sins as murder or witchcraft. Sometimes, it is manifested when you choose to stay in bed on Sunday mornings or when you respond in anger toward your spouse. Your flesh is at enmity with the Spirit of God within you.

We need change because we each reside in a fleshly tabernacle; the flesh is in opposition to the life of Christ. That is why Paul said in Ephesians 4:22–24, *"That ye put off concerning the former conversation the old man, which is corrupt according to the deceitful lusts; And be renewed in the spirit of your mind; And that ye put on the new man, which after God is created in righteousness and true holiness."*

We are often guilty of having selfish notions. We think we know what is best for our lives, and we tend to lean on our own understanding. Proverbs 14:12 says, *"There is a way which seemeth right unto a man, but the end thereof are the ways of death."* Because of our selfish notions, our natural tendency is to have it "our way." We want just enough of the "God thing" to appease our family and to portray spiritual respectability to those around us.

Friend, God is looking for Christians who will come alive in Christ and say, "Where He leads me, I will follow." Isaiah 53:6 says, *"All we like sheep have gone astray...."* What a tremendous illustration of the human race! We want to go our own way, but we need to confess our need for a Christ-like change. We must humble ourselves and recognize our tendency to wander, to fail, and to fall. We must admit before God that we need and desire His change in our hearts.

You may be thinking that change is not possible. You may have stopped fighting the battle long ago. You may have given up hope that you can truly change. Friend, don't become discouraged. God has made change possible within you, and recognizing that need is the first step to true change. Are you willing to agree with God regarding the need for change in your life? Are you willing to admit your need to grow?

Agreeing to change requires humility. It may mean changing thought patterns, getting up in the morning and reevaluating who you are in Christ, or being more faithful to church. You must say, "Lord, I have not arrived. I am not where I should be in my walk with You, and I am willing to change."

*Likewise, ye younger, submit yourselves unto the elder.
Yea, all of you be subject one to another, and be clothed
with humility: for God resisteth the proud, and giveth
grace to the humble.*—1 PETER 5:5

When we humble ourselves, God will give us the grace we
need for change. Our potential lies not in our *ability*, but in
our *humility*. We must admit to God that our flesh is weak, but
through His strength, we can continue to change to become more
like Him day by day.

We Must Reckon that the Lord Is Right

*Knowing this, that our old man is crucified with
him, that the body of sin might be destroyed, that
henceforth we should not serve sin. For he that is dead
is freed from sin. Now if we be dead with Christ, we
believe that we shall also live with him: Knowing that
Christ being raised from the dead dieth no more; death
hath no more dominion over him. For in that he died,
he died unto sin once: but in that he liveth, he liveth
unto God. Likewise reckon ye also yourselves to be
dead indeed unto sin, but alive unto God through Jesus
Christ our Lord.*—ROMANS 6:6–11

Now that we understand the weakness of our flesh and the
need for change in our lives, we must realize that God's Word is
true. It is one thing for me to say that the old man is crucified,
but to reckon the old man dead is entirely different! The word
reckon in verse eleven means "to set to one's account; to credit, or
to acknowledge." God wants me to acknowledge that the claims
of His Word are true and that His truth can help me experience
victory—whether or not it seems humanly possible.

We are faced with similar reckonings every day of our lives. For example, when you see a speed limit sign, you have a reckoning: Is this warning true and needful? Some of us will see this sign and reckon it as law. We will choose to obey the warning. Others of us will not reckon or heed its message.

God has given each of us as believers this truth to reckon: Satan was defeated at the Cross, and our old nature was made new in Christ. We can either reckon this as truth and live a life set apart unto Him, or we can refuse to acknowledge the victory wrought by Jesus on the Cross. We must choose to put the power of the Cross to our account. We must reckon ourselves alive unto Christ each day.

This powerful reckoning requires faith in the Word of God. First John 5:4 says, *"For whatsoever is born of God overcometh the world: and this is the victory that overcometh the world, even our faith."* Do you have faith that the victory has already been purchased and that you can live a life set apart to God and His Word? Do you believe that it is possible? Do you accept God's promise as truth or do you believe the constant lies of Satan— the constant accusations of the enemy telling you this kind of spiritual life is impossible?

Brother Lester Roloff was a great preacher in the twentieth century. He pastored People's Baptist Church in Corpus Christi, Texas, and he also founded several children's homes. It seemed that he was always facing battles with the state over orphanage licenses. He felt that these homes should not be licensed, because they were part of his church's ministry. One day, while he was in the midst of a court battle, the opposing attorney began to say, "Mr. Roloff, you are nothing but a rebel rouser—a preacher looking for a fight." He began to curse and yell at this man of God.

At the end of the day, the unsaved attorney felt sorry for the way he had spoken to Brother Roloff. He went to apologize and said, "Reverend, what I did today is just what I do. It is part of my job. It's nothing personal."

Mr. Roloff, who believed in the Word of God and reckoned himself dead to sin and alive unto Christ, looked at that unsaved attorney and said, "You can't offend a dead man." "What do you mean?" the attorney asked. "In Jesus Christ, I am dead to sin; I am dead to self; and I am alive unto God. Because I am dead to sin and criticism, you can't hurt me." Lester Roloff had learned how to have victory in the Christian life. He had learned to reckon himself dead to sin and alive to Jesus Christ.

If you are going to live for God, you must reckon His Word to be true and needful in your life. You must accept, by faith, that victory is possible. You must claim God's true promise and acknowledge that He is right! When you understand and accept the power of God's Word in your life, change becomes more than a possibility—it becomes a reality!

We Must Yield to the Spirit of God

Admitting the need for change and accepting the truth of God's Word leads us to a decision. This truth becomes a reality through daily yielding to the Holy Spirit of God. Romans 6:13 states, *"Neither yield ye your members as instruments of unrighteousness unto sin: but yield yourselves unto God, as those that are alive from the dead, and your members as instruments of righteousness unto God."* Being yielded is a choice. We can yield to unrighteousness, or we can yield our lives to follow God. One author said, "Just two choices on the shelf—serving God or serving self."

The key to living a sanctified life is not found in a twelve-step program. Living for God comes down to one simple choice each day—am I willing to reckon myself dead unto sin and to yield myself alive to the Holy Spirit?

Many years ago, after I had finished preaching our Sunday evening message, a man, whom I had met through a church ministry, came to speak to me. His body was literally shaking as he said, "Pastor, I have a problem, and I need help. I am addicted to cocaine." For several months it was my pleasure to provide daily contact with him. We would read Scripture together, and I would pray for God's power in helping him overcome this sin. He said that as long as I met with him daily, it would help him experience victory. The accountability helped him stay disciplined.

One day I asked him, "What if God would meet with you each day? Would that help?" He said, "Of course." "Good," I said, "Because I can't meet with you tomorrow, but God can!" Throughout the next few months, I was not able to meet with him on a daily basis, but the Lord did! Day by day, that man walked with Jesus Christ, Who is the same yesterday, today, and forever. In Hebrews 13:5, He said, "…*I will never leave thee, nor forsake thee*." It was the presence and power of Jesus Christ that ultimately enabled my friend to overcome his addiction.

Sometimes, we blame our failures in life on a lack of discipline. What we often call a lack of discipline is really a lack of devotion. It is a lack of yielding ourselves to the power of God. If we will yield ourselves to Jesus, He will give us the sustaining grace to become more like Him. He will supernaturally empower us and enable us to experience the change we so desperately need.

Romans 6:15–16 says, "*What then? shall we sin, because we are not under the law, but under grace? God forbid. Know ye not, that to whom ye yield yourselves servants to obey, his servants ye are to whom ye obey; whether of sin unto death, or of obedience unto righteousness?*"

This passage helps us understand that a life yielded to Christ equals a life conformed to His image. You become a servant to whom or what you choose to yield. If you yield yourself to drugs, sex, and wrong friends, you become their servant, but if you yield yourself to God, you become His servant unto righteousness.

Several years ago, our church sent a group of young people on a missions trip to the Philippines. One evening, the missions team leader was standing in a hotel lobby when the manager approached him. He immediately asked him, "Are you people Christians?" When our group leader answered him, the manager proceeded to ask, "Sir, what is the difference between a Christian and a Catholic?" The leader began to witness to him, and a few moments later, that hotel manager asked Jesus Christ to be his Saviour. This dear man in the Philippines noticed something different about our group. Why? Because our church believes that the grace of God is not a license to sin, rather it is the finished work of Christ showing itself evident in our daily lives.

Galatians 6:7–8 states, *"Be not deceived; God is not mocked: for whatsoever a man soweth, that shall he also reap. For he that soweth to his flesh shall of the flesh reap corruption; but he that soweth to the Spirit shall of the Spirit reap life everlasting."* When we reckon ourselves dead to sin and alive to Jesus Christ, we are sowing in the Spirit, and we will bear the fruit of true change that pleases Christ.

If our lives remain yielded to God, we cannot constantly feed fleshly appetites. Romans 8:13 says, *"For if ye live after the flesh, ye shall die: but if ye through the Spirit do mortify the deeds of the body, ye shall live."*

There is no greater life than one that is yielded to God. Yielding to God will lead to a changed life that reflects His grace. As we recognize our need for change, and as we yield our lives to Him, His grace will lead us into a more holy life—a life conforming to the image of Christ.

Have you admitted the need for change in your life? Are you willing to look to God's Word for help and to yield yourself to Him and His will for you? Becoming like Christ begins with humbling yourself and admitting your need for Him. Why not take a moment right now to bow your head and heart before the Lord? Confess to Him that you are helpless without Him, and tell Him you long for the true change that only His power can bring. If you will admit your need, believe His Word, and yield to His Spirit, you are on the road to change already! The journey ahead is going to be one of true transformation by God's grace.

CHAPTER TEN

The Way of Renewal
Philippians 2:12–13

D r. Harry Ironside was speaking before an assembly one day when he noticed a man writing something on a card. He then brought the card up to where Dr. Ironside was lecturing. This man was Arthur Lewis, an agnostic lecturer, and he proposed the following challenge: a debate on the subject of "Agnosticism vs. Christianity." Dr. Ironside read the card aloud to the audience and then said, "I accept your challenge under these conditions: First, you must promise to bring with you to the platform one man who was once an outcast and a slave to sinful habits, but who heard you or some other infidel lecture on agnosticism and was helped to the point that he cast away his sins, became a new man, and is today a respected member of society... all because of your unbelief!

"Second, you must agree to bring with you one woman who was once lost to all purity and goodness, but who can now testify that agnosticism came to her rescue while deep in sin and implanted in her poor heart a hatred of impurity and a love of holiness, causing her to become chaste and upright... all through a disbelief in the Bible!

"Now sir," he continued, "if you will agree, I promise to be there with one hundred such men and women, once just lost souls, who have heard the Gospel of the grace of God and have found new life and joy in Jesus Christ our Saviour. Will you accept my terms?" Lewis walked away in silence.

The Christian life is primarily about a relationship with God. In this day, when there is an abundance of agnostic reasoning and focus on self-help, you must recognize that God is the reason you are here today, and He is the One who will transform you into the image of His Son.

The primary purpose for your life is not to learn more about yourself or other people; you are here to know God and to become like His Son! Man only functions well when he is in good fellowship with his Creator. As you learn more about Him, your life will begin to change and you will experience spiritual renewal and sanctification.

A lady once said, "I finally got in touch with my inner self, and she's just as confused as I am!" Getting to know yourself and others better will not bring a life change. The key to a renewed life is getting to know your Creator. The Apostle Paul said in Acts 17:28, *"For in him we live, and move, and have our being...."* In essence, Paul was saying, "My whole life is in Christ." When we experience real fellowship with God, all of the other relationships in life will be renewed.

The Desire for Renewal

Spiritual renewal does not come naturally to us. We often fight our flesh and those things that are displeasing to God. Where will this desire to know God come from? Philippians 2:13 says, *"For it is God which worketh in you both to will and to do of his good pleasure."* God places within each of His children a desire to know Him. If I have a desire to know God, it is because of His work in me. If you know Christ, then somewhere within you, God has placed a desire to know Him and to be close to Him.

Romans 7:18 states, *"For I know that in me (that is, in my flesh,) dwelleth no good thing: for to will is present with me; but how to perform that which is good I find not."* Paul is saying, "I have a will and a desire to do right, but my flesh hinders me from performing that which is good."

Spiritual renewal is the work of God from the inside out. It begins with God, and continues as we are yielded to Him. God does give us the "will" to know Him, yet we must follow that will with a personal response. Jeremiah 31:3 says, *"The LORD hath appeared of old unto me, saying, Yea, I have loved thee with an everlasting love: therefore with lovingkindness have I drawn thee."* When we were saved, God called us unto Him and gave us a desire to know Him. He draws us to Himself, but leaves us the choice of whether to respond or not.

A French proverb states, "A good meal ought to begin with hunger." Have you noticed how everything tastes good when your stomach is empty? It is hard to enjoy food when you are already full. As Christians, we must empty our hearts of any fleshly desires, and we must hunger to know Him. He will satisfy our need every time. Spiritual renewal and effective worship begin with a hunger and desire for God and His Word.

Not only does God give us a will, but Philippians 2:13 says that He will *"do of his good pleasure."* God gives us the desire to know Him, and then He accomplishes His will through our lives. Galatians 5:16–17 illustrates this new nature of the believer. *"This I say then, Walk in the Spirit, and ye shall not fulfil the lust of the flesh. For the flesh lusteth against the Spirit, and the Spirit against the flesh: and these are contrary the one to the other: so that ye cannot do the things that ye would."*

The Holy Spirit gives us the desire to know God, attend church, and witness to a lost friend. The question is, "Will I follow God, or will I let my flesh control me? Will I yield to the Holy Spirit's working in my life?"

The Bible tells us how we can follow God's will in Romans 8:14, 16: *"For as many as are led by the Spirit of God, they are the sons of God. The Spirit itself beareth witness with our spirit, that we are the children of God."* God's Holy Spirit gives us the will to do right and to become like Christ. He desires to bring us to spiritual maturity. The flesh wants to bring us back to the old friends, wrong music, and addictive habits, but God says, "I have a will for your life. My desire is that you would be conformed to the image of my Son as you are led by the Spirit of God."

Many times you can recognize a Christian by his lifestyle. You can tell that he is following the leadership of the Holy Spirit. God did not save us so that we could go back to our sinful habits; He saved us so that we could follow the Spirit's leading in our everyday lives. If you have never felt a desire to grow in godliness, it would be wise to examine if you have ever become His child. Those who are truly His children will have a hunger and a desire to know Him more deeply.

Matthew 5:6 says, *"Blessed are they which do hunger and thirst after righteousness: for they shall be filled."* God does not create a desire that He does not intend to satisfy. One preacher put it this way, "God puts a hole in the heart of man that only Jesus can fill." If you truly desire to know God, you will be filled. Any attempt to solve this God-given desire in another way is doomed to fail!

The Samaritan woman in John 4 is a good example of this truth. She had been married several times and was now living in a sinful relationship outside of marriage. Jesus Christ approached her and began speaking about water that would fill her empty life forever. He told her that she had been trying to find satisfaction in other ways, but had never really known God or the way of salvation. That day the Samaritan woman believed on Jesus Christ, she experienced restoration and spiritual renewal.

God has placed in every person a desire to know Him more. When we truly seek to know Him and to serve Him, this desire will be fulfilled. Only when we follow after Him will we be able to become like Christ and experience His joy!

Seeking for Renewal

Seek the LORD, and his strength: seek his face evermore.—PSALM 105:4

Someone who has a God-given desire for renewal will seek spiritual renewal through the Holy Spirit. Deuteronomy 4:29 says, *"But if from thence thou shalt seek the LORD thy God, thou shalt find him, if thou seek him with all thy heart and with all thy soul."* Let's observe two ways we must seek this kind of renewal in our lives today.

Spiritual growth and renewal first requires diligent study and determination. Some Christians believe that the Christian life is a party—nothing but fun and games. They are apathetic toward the Lord, because they are passionate about seeking other things. Do you have a passion to know God? Are you seeking Him? The Christian life is not effortless. It requires something. It requires that we seek God diligently, and He promises to reward our seeking!

Every man and woman was created as a passionate being, but they cannot be passionate about both God and the world. Matthew 6:24 says, *"No man can serve two masters: for either he will hate the one, and love the other; or else he will hold to the one, and despise the other. Ye cannot serve God and mammon."*

For this reason, the Apostle Paul is a great example to us; his overwhelming goal in life was to know God. He says in Philippians 3:10, *"That I may know him, and the power of his resurrection, and the fellowship of his sufferings, being made conformable unto his death."*

Second, spiritual renewal requires devotion. Many times we lack discipline in the Christian life because we have no affection for the things of God. Deuteronomy 6:5 says, *"And thou shalt love the LORD thy God with all thine heart, and with all thy soul, and with all thy might."* The reason we don't spend time in God's Word is not a busy schedule or lack of organization, it is because we do not love the God of the Word.

Throughout the years, my wife has written me many letters. Sometimes she'll leave a sticky note on my bathroom mirror, or she'll even place toothpaste on my toothbrush. When I see the evidences of her love, I think to myself, "Wow! This is going to be a good day!" When she leaves a letter on my dresser, I don't say, "Well, I think I'll read that letter when I get home tonight." No, I tear it open that moment! I am glad to know that my wife loves me with devotion.

We are living in a busy day, and sometimes God gets crowded out of our schedule. We need to renew our desire to seek God with determination and devotion, and we must give Him first priority in our lives every day. Psalm 34:10 says, *"The young lions do lack, and suffer hunger: but they that seek the LORD shall not want any good thing."* God says, "I'm still here. If you will seek Me, I will give you what you need." The emphasis is not about seeking more principles; most of us know more principles than we care to apply. It is about seeking a person—Jesus Christ.

Many years ago, a hymnist wrote *Take Time to Be Holy*. The lyrics say,

> Take time to be holy, the world rushes on,
> Spend much time in secret with Jesus alone.

By looking to Jesus like Him thou shalt be,
Thy friends and thy conduct His likeness shall see.

Some may respond to those words with questions such as, "Who has the time?" and, "Who wants to be holy?" My friend, spiritual renewal is about becoming like Christ, and He is holy! We must make time every day to meet with Him and to become more holy.

Wouldn't it be a wonderful thing if every one of us would take time to be holy—if we would spend time in God's Word and admit our need for Him? What a testimony it would be if your coworkers said, "There is something going on in his life that I want."

In Luke 24:32, as the disciples walked along the Emmaus road with Jesus, they said to each other, "...*Did not our heart burn within us, while he talked with us by the way, and while he opened to us the scriptures?*"

I believe God wants to warm our hearts through daily fellowship with Him. If we will be renewed and sanctified to become more like Christ, we must follow that God-given desire to seek His presence in our lives.

Abiding in Renewal

First, God gives me the desire to know Him and to be led by His Spirit. That desire causes me to seek the Lord. He says, "If you seek Me, you will find Me." I've found Him, and I can say, "Praise God, I am His, and He is mine." Once I have entered that place of fellowship, my heart's desire is to stay there—to abide with Him continually.

The carnal Christian spends ten minutes with God on Saturday or an hour with Him on Sunday and then goes back to his wicked world Monday through Friday. He goes to church to get a small dose of God and lives like the world the rest of the week. We shouldn't compartmentalize our relationship with Christ in this way. God should be at the center of everything that we do in life.

The gift of fellowship with Christ is not merely for a Sunday morning; it is available every day. John 15:4 states, *"Abide in me, and I in you. As the branch cannot bear fruit of itself, except it abide in the vine; no more can ye, except ye abide in me."* God wants us to spend time in close fellowship with Him on a daily basis.

A married couple may abide in the same house together. They may have common goals and mutual interests, yet that does not mean they are experiencing oneness and spiritual intimacy. God says that it is not enough for us to attend church and have mutual religious beliefs; He wants us to enjoy continual intimacy with Him. He wants our fellowship with Him to be open and clear. Who are we kidding when we feel anger or think impure thoughts? God knows everything. Why not confess your sin, acknowledge His presence, and walk through life in open fellowship with Him?

As we abide with God, He wants us also to experience joy. Even as a married couple enjoys common interests, God desires to be one person with us. When you love someone, your greatest joy is when he or she experiences joy.

There is joy in living for Jesus Christ and fulfilling His purpose for your life. Fun is found in a heart of joy that comes only from Jesus Christ. First John 1:3–4 says, *"That which we have seen and heard declare we unto you, that ye also may have fellowship with us: and truly our fellowship is with the Father, and with his Son Jesus Christ. And these things write we unto you, that your joy may be full."*

The man who is living for the devil has no joy. He has to have another drink just to soothe his conscience, but we can walk in joy every day knowing that there is a God who loves us—knowing that we will spend an eternity with Him! We can abide in this renewing relationship every moment of every day. He invites us to abide in Him constantly, to include Him in every decision, call on Him for every need, trust in Him for every provision, and follow Him in every circumstance. He desires to be with us all day long, constantly transforming, renewing, and shaping us into the image of His Son, yet He leaves the choice to us. God will not force us to spend time with Him.

Salvation is more than an escape from Hell; it is living a transformed and spiritually renewed life here on this earth. You need renewal today and every day. You need God's strength to change you. God can renew the believer who is spiritually empty if he will desire, seek, and abide with Him! God promises strength and encouragement to the Christian who will follow the pathway of spiritual renewal. Friend, have you been renewed spiritually today? If not, I encourage you to take time right now to seek God and to renew your spirit in Him.

CHAPTER ELEVEN

Changed by the Glory of God
2 Corinthians 3:17–4:2

A man found a butterfly chrysalis and excitedly began observing its metamorphosis. One day, a small opening appeared. The man sat and watched the butterfly for several hours as it struggled to force its body through the little hole. Then the butterfly seemed to stop making any progress. It appeared as if it had no strength to go further, so the man decided to help. He took a pair of scissors and snipped off the remaining bit of the cocoon-like covering. The butterfly emerged easily, but it had a swollen body and small, shriveled wings. The man continued to watch the butterfly, because he expected that at any moment the wings would enlarge and expand to support the body, which would contract in time.

Neither happened. In fact, the butterfly spent the rest of its life crawling around with a swollen body and shriveled wings. It was never able to fly. In his kindness and haste, the man did not understand that the restricting shell and the struggle required for the butterfly to get through the tiny opening was God's way of forcing fluid from the body of the butterfly into its wings, so that it would be ready for flight once it achieved its freedom.

If you are going to become like Christ, then you must experience this dynamic change. God's will is not only to bring you into the image of His Son someday in Heaven; His will is to conform you progressively through your walk with Him today.

Second Corinthians 3:17–18 gives insight into this truth: *"Now the Lord is that Spirit: and where the Spirit of the Lord is, there is liberty. But we all, with open face beholding as in a glass the glory of the Lord, are changed into the same image from glory to glory, even as by the Spirit of the Lord."* When Paul looked into the Word of God and came face to face with the Lord, his life was completely changed. The word *changed* in verse 18 means to "metamorphose." In other words, Paul said, "When I came into contact with Jesus Christ and accepted Him as my Saviour, my life was changed."

I remember going soulwinning with my daughter, Danielle, one Saturday several years ago. We knocked on the door of one residence with the hope of telling them about Jesus Christ. They graciously invited us into their home. I will never forget that visit. There was loud rock and roll music playing, and the man seemed rough with a long ponytail and earrings. I soon discovered that he did not have a religious background.

After several minutes of casual conversation, he kindly turned the music down, and I was able to ask him this question: "If you were to die today, are you sure that Heaven would be your home?" He thought about it for a moment and then said, "I don't know if I would go to Heaven." After thirty or forty minutes of sharing the Gospel with him, he accepted Jesus Christ as his Saviour.

It was a blessing to see him and his wife get baptized at church the next morning and then watch as they began to grow in the Lord. After a Sunday evening service, I asked him to accompany me to a church in Los Angeles where I would be preaching the following evening. I remember watching his jaw drop as he looked down at his rough appearance. "You want me to go with you?" he asked incredulously. "Sure," I said, "You need to hear the songs of the faith and be around the people of God. I would love to have you go with me. I'll pick you up tomorrow evening at five o'clock."

The next day, I pulled up in front of his house and honked the horn. Coming out of the house was a man I didn't recognize. This fellow had a very short haircut and a hole in his ear where an earring used to be. He was wearing a three-piece business suit and carrying a Bible. As we drove to Los Angeles, I could not help but think about the amazing God we serve. Was it the discipleship class or the church service that made the difference in this man? Neither. It was the presence of the Holy Spirit in his life. He was "metamorphosed" (or changed) by the glory of the Almighty God.

If you will take a moment and think back to the time when you accepted Jesus Christ as your Saviour, you too will realize that a change took place in your life that day. The tragedy for most Christians is that the growth process stops five or ten years after salvation. The whole premise of this book is that God wants the dynamic work that took place on the day of salvation to continue throughout your Christian life.

The Christian life is a spiritual life, and it is important to understand that only the Holy Spirit can bring inner change. This truth is explained in verse seventeen, *"Now the Lord is that Spirit: and where the Spirit of the Lord is, there is liberty."* Second Corinthians 6 speaks about Moses and his descendants and how they had not known spiritual liberty; they did not experience the presence of the Holy Spirit in the same abiding way as believers did after Pentecost.

When you receive Christ as your Saviour, the veil of blindness is lifted, and God brings about change through His Spirit and His Holy Word. No one who is exposed to the glory of God as revealed by His Spirit can remain the same. God will change your life as it is exposed to His glory and as you open your heart to Him.

When a sinner comes face to face with Jesus Christ and trusts Him as Saviour, I believe this is a faith encounter with the wonderful glory of God. The Bible says in John 1:14, *"And the Word was made flesh, and dwelt among us, (and we beheld his glory, the glory as of the only begotten of the Father,) full of grace and truth."* When Christ saved us, we had the privilege of entering into the presence and the life-changing glory of Almighty God.

This lesson is not about outward conformity but about inner change. It is about beholding the "glory" of the Lord through the Word of God and being inwardly changed by His Spirit. The reason there is joy and anticipation in the heart of a new believer is that the Spirit has taken up permanent residence. God wants to change the new believer day by day by the pricking of the Holy Spirit. Some people are Alka-Seltzer Christians—they hit the baptistry then fizzle out. God's desire is for you to continually experience dynamic change and growth in your life, and He desires that change to be generated by your daily walk with Him—your daily glimpse of His glory. Friend, when you experience God's glory, you cannot walk away unchanged. Entering His presence will transform your life from the inside like nothing else can! Let's discover the amazing part that God's glory plays in helping us to become like Christ.

Experiencing His Glory Is Humbling

I heard about an employer who was not getting any respect from his employees. In fact, everybody seemed to make fun of him behind his back. He became extremely frustrated. One day, he went to a sign shop and had a sign made that said, "I am the boss." He put that large sign on the wall of his office. Later that day, he went to lunch. Upon his return, he saw a small sign taped under the larger one. It said, "Your wife wants her sign back."

Sometimes we all have degrading experiences. Don't misunderstand. God's glory is not degrading, but it is humbling. Nothing is more humbling than comparing our position as lost sinners to the glory of Jesus Christ.

When I accepted Christ as my Saviour, I came to the realization that I had fallen short of God's glory. Romans 3:23 says, *"For all have sinned, and come short of the glory of God."* The psalmist accurately describes this truth in Psalm 8:3–4. *"When I consider thy heavens, the work of thy fingers, the moon and the stars, which thou hast ordained; What is man, that thou art mindful of him? and the son of man, that thou visitest him?"* When we consider God's power and magnificence as the Creator and Saviour of this world, what is man?

Our culture is continuing in a downward spiral toward the depths of depravity. What a humbling experience it is to realize that God, in His glory, loves us in spite of such outward perversion and sin in our world today! Romans 5:8–9 states, *"But God commendeth his love toward us, in that, while we were yet sinners, Christ died for us. Much more then, being now justified by his blood, we shall be saved from wrath through him."* If you have never accepted Christ's gift of salvation, you must come to a point of true humility—a realization of your position as a lost sinner and of Christ's position as the Saviour of this world.

This humbling effect will draw us into willing obedience to Christ. Our Christian lives will genuinely respond to God and submit to His will, not merely put up the right outward appearance.

Experiencing His Glory Is Emotional

As Bible-believing Christians, we do not move from emotion to doctrine, but from doctrine to emotion. Yet, God created emotions, and there is no doubt that He can use our emotions for His purposes in our lives.

At the moment of salvation and throughout the Christian life, God encourages, renews, and changes our hearts. The heart is the innermost part of our spiritual being—the seat of our emotions. When we open God's Word and apply its truths to our hearts, it brings emotional change.

I believe when a man enters into the glory of God's grace, he experiences true joy. First Peter 1:8 says, "*Whom having not seen, ye love; in whom, though now ye see him not, yet believing, ye rejoice with joy unspeakable and full of glory.*"

I recently received a letter from a man who had come back to the Lord after many years of backsliding. One sentence said, "I cannot describe the joy of God in my heart. Each time I hear the Word of God preached, and I see people responding to the truth, tears of joy run down my cheeks." God's glory has made a huge emotional difference in this man's life.

A believer who is basking in God's glory will not only experience joy, he will also know inward peace. Paul said to the church at Philippi in Philippians 4:7, "*And the peace of God, which passeth all understanding, shall keep your hearts and minds through Christ Jesus.*"

During our first year of ministry in Lancaster, we had a small group of faithful members. One of them was an elderly lady named Clara Daugherty. After she became ill, I would often visit her at her apartment. On one occasion, I asked if she had any needs that our church could supply. She said, "Pastor Chappell, I'm satisfied."

How can a woman with poor health, no family, and no money be content? Clara Daugherty spent time in the presence of God—she walked with Him and meditated on His Word. She recognized that the joy and peace of God was not found in her surroundings but in the Person who had changed her life. She was able to say, *"O taste and see that the LORD is good: blessed is the man that trusteth in him"* (Psalm 34:8).

As believers, we are often discontented, driven, and frantic, because we have not spent sufficient time basking in the glory of God. That is why Jesus could say in Matthew 11:28–30, *"Come unto me, all ye that labour and are heavy laden, and I will give you rest. Take my yoke upon you, and learn of me; for I am meek and lowly in heart: and ye shall find rest unto your souls. For my yoke is easy, and my burden is light."*

Sometimes soul-rest escapes us, because we simply do not come before our Saviour and spend time with Him. We do not walk with Him in fellowship, and thus we do not come into His life-changing glory. When we experience His glory, we will find the rest that our soul needs. His peace will rule in our hearts.

Friend, have you experienced His glory today? Are your frustrations showing, or are God's peace and power guiding and shaping your life? Spending time with God will transform you emotionally and others will notice the difference!

Experiencing His Glory Is Compelling

There is something compelling about coming into the presence of the Almighty God. I am greatly encouraged when I think about my position as a child of God. My heart is filled with joy and peace, and I feel compelled to serve the One Who has done so much for me. His glory will provoke a response. It will call me to action for Christ and for His church.

When we stand in the presence of God, we will be compelled to serve Him. When we stand in His presence, we will be filled with peace and joy. We will be "re-fueled" for the Lord's service. We will be able to say, "I want to do something for this God who has done something for me."

If you are doing something for God because of obligation or peer pressure, you won't do it very long, and you won't discover the great joy that can be found in serving Christ with a pure heart. But, if you are compelled to serve God because of His presence in your life, even the most menial tasks become a delight. Isaiah 6:8 says, *"Also I heard the voice of the Lord, saying, Whom shall I send, and who will go for us? Then said I, Here am I; send me."*

Many times the reason we don't want to serve is that we are not spending time in the presence of God's glory. When God is really a presence in our lives, we won't attempt to do as little as possible for Christ. We will seek to obey Him completely and to do all that He would lead us to do.

The effect of the glory of God in your life will be true revival in your heart. Your response to His Word should be, "This humbles me; this brings peace to me; and this compels me to serve Christ!"

God's glory will also compel you to know Him. If you think on your salvation and what He did for you that day, you will instantly have a greater desire to know Him. When you stand in the presence of God, you will be compelled to seek Him and know Him more intimately.

His glory will also compel others to glorify Him. Matthew 5:16 says, *"Let your light so shine before men, that they may see your good works, and glorify your Father which is in heaven."* Friend, we don't want them to see our good works and glorify *us*, we want them to see our Father and glorify *Him*. This is the true desire of someone who has been in the presence of Jesus Christ.

When was the last time the glory of His Word and the glory of His presence brought significant change into your life? When was the last time you found renewed peace, renewed joy, and a compelling desire to serve Him as a result of spending time in His Word?

God, through His Spirit and by His Word, brings change. No one who is exposed to the glory of God, as revealed by His Spirit, can remain the same! Being changed by His glory is not about outward conformity, but about an inward change. It is about beholding the "glory" of the Lord through the Word of the Lord and being inwardly changed by the Spirit of the Lord.

The psalmist said it perfectly when he wrote, *"What is man, that thou art mindful of him? and the son of man, that thou visitest him?"* (Psalm 8:4). God wants you to be changed into His likeness. He wants your life to be a testimony of His power by being changed by His glory.

Friend, are you truly seeking to be changed by His glory? It is an amazing thing to be able to come into the presence of the Lord. May we not take it for granted. We have the answer to all of life's problems, if we would only seek His face. We have the source of all peace and strength, if we would only enter His presence. We have the power of God on our side, if we will only bask in His glory. Are you humbled? Do you have peace and joy? Are you compelled to serve the Saviour? If not, seek the glory of God right now. Pray, and ask Him to change you to be more like Him by His glory.

CHAPTER TWELVE

Developing the Mind of Christ
Philippians 2:5–8

Every year, I look forward to the first day of school at
Lancaster Baptist School. It is fun to watch the parents,
especially the mothers of kindergartners, as they bring their
kids to school. We have a special crying room prepared just for
them, and they come in with Kleenex in one hand and a camera
in the other. Of course, I always enjoy this scene, because I do not
want to think about the growth of my own four children.

I have often stated to our school parents, "The goal of
Christian education is to develop the mind of Christ." Jonathan
Witherspoon, the sixth president of Princeton once stated, "Cursed
be all learning that is not subservient to the Cross of Christ." There
is no greater wisdom—no greater mindset than the mind of Christ.

To have the mind of Christ you must think spiritually. I know
this truth sounds very basic, but think with me for a moment. God
says to us, "I want you to have a heavenly mind." The Bible says in
Romans 8:6, *"For to be carnally minded is death; but to be spiritually*

minded is life and peace." To be carnally minded—to think like the carnal man is death.

Why do Christians resist the command of God to have the mind of Christ? The mind of man and the mind of Christ are completely opposite. If you have His mind, you will experience life, peace, and His power. You will know His will for your life. Romans 8:7-8 go on to say, *"Because the carnal mind is enmity against God: for it is not subject to the law of God, neither indeed can be. So then they that are in the flesh cannot please God."*

Developing the mind of Christ is not only a matter of your thought process, but also a matter of your heart attitude. Philippians 2:5 states, *"Let this mind be in you, which was also in Christ Jesus."* This verse admonishes us to let the mind of Christ—His humility and lowliness—flow through our lives. This is an assault on our natural human autonomy—our desire to control our lives. This goes against our nature to be our own authority.

To become like Christ, you must think like He thinks. You must allow Him to dictate your thoughts, your desires, and your emotions. Let's discover what the mind of Christ is really all about.

His Position

For you to comprehend the mind of Christ—the depths of His love and compassion—you must first understand His position as the Son of God. It is one thing for us to walk more humbly and godly, but imagine the condescension of Jesus Christ, as He became man for us. Philippians 2:6 says, *"Who, being in the form of God, thought it not robbery to be equal with God."*

The Bible tells us that Jesus is the eternally pre-existent Son of God. The word *being* in verse 6 is not only referencing His state in this life, but also His existence prior to His appearance in the flesh. John 1:14 tells us, *"And the Word was made flesh, and dwelt among us, (and we beheld his glory, the glory as of the only begotten of the Father,) full of grace and truth."*

Did you catch that? The Word was made flesh. *"In the beginning was the Word, and the Word was with God, and the Word was God"* (John 1:1). These verses are speaking of the living Word—the Son of God, Jesus Christ. His existence did not begin in the manger at Bethlehem; His existence was from eternity past. Christ declared in John 10:30, *"I and my Father are one"*—in knowledge, power, and all of God's attributes.

Not only is Jesus the pre-existent Son of God, He was also God in the flesh—*"being in the form of God."* The word *form* means "the outward expression of the inward nature." Jesus was the outward expression of God. When Jesus Christ came to earth in the flesh, He revealed God personally to all mankind. Hebrews 1:3 speaks of Jesus, *"Who being the brightness of his glory, and the express image of his person, and upholding all things by the word of his power, when he had by himself purged our sins, sat down on the right hand of the Majesty on high."*

In Hebrews 1:3, Jesus was high and lifted up, yet the mind of Christ is an attitude that says, "Though I am at the right hand of God and I have all power to create and raise up life, I cannot keep My privileges for Myself; I must use them for others."

"Others" is a key word in the vocabulary of the Christian who will become like Christ. For example, the Bible says to prefer one another, bear one another's burdens, and admonish one another. A Christ-like Christian thinks of others, regardless of his position or status. Jesus Christ, who was high and lifted up, humbled Himself to meet the needs of others. Have you developed the mind of Christ by preferring others?

To have the mind of Christ is to use your position to serve. Jesus used His eternal power and Godhead to rescue humanity! Are you using your abilities, your position, and your status in this life to serve others? Are you sharing the message of Christ with others? When you begin thinking like Christ, you will use everything at your disposal to honor God and to serve others.

His Decision

Jesus Christ decided to humble Himself to meet the needs of sinners. He was willing to meet the needs of a spiritually sick and dying race of people. Philippians 2:7 states, *"But made himself of no reputation, and took upon him the form of a servant, and was made in the likeness of men."*

Jesus shows us the most perfect example of humility the world has ever seen. The Gospel of Luke tells us that Jesus allowed Himself to be overshadowed by the Holy Spirit. He was miraculously born in a lowly stable to a carpenter and his wife.

Christ knew how He would be born. He knew that He would leave the splendor of Heaven for a simple upbringing on earth. He had the right and the authority to be born as the King of kings—to be wrapped in the finest linens and to have all the glory and honor He was due! Yet, He made a choice to be *"of no reputation…and was made in the likeness of men."* He did not reduce His deity, but He restrained it, so that we might be saved.

The central message of Philippians 2:5–8 is, "The way up is down." In the Christian life, we must descend into greatness. We must come to a place where we say, "Lord, help me to become more like You. If that means humbling myself and losing a promotion, if that means missing out on something great in man's eyes, Lord, I just want to become more conformed to Your image." Aren't you glad that Christ decided to humble Himself and die for us?

Jesus' example teaches us that greatness is not measured by "self-will" but by "self-abandonment." James 4:10 tells us, *"Humble yourselves in the sight of the Lord, and he shall lift you up."* The example of Jesus' humility is a tremendous challenge to me. As I seek to become more like Christ, I don't want to worry about how I am being perceived. I want to focus on being an effective servant for the Saviour.

The second part of Philippians 2:7 says that Jesus "...*took upon him the form of a servant...*." In this day of upward mobility, negotiations, and climbing the corporate ladder, the world is not accustomed to this type of "downward mobility." I firmly believe that if we would exhibit this Christ-like spirit in our marriages, families, and to our coworkers, it would have a profound impact! Jesus Christ would be clearly seen in our lives.

May we wake up tomorrow and say, "Lord, help me to take on the form of a servant today. Help me to be willing to do the tasks that no one else wants to do." God will bless a humble servant's heart.

One of the greatest illustrations of Jesus' servitude is found in John 13 when He washed His disciples' feet. In this passage, He exemplified what it means to be empty of self and to serve others with humility:

> *Jesus knowing that the Father had given all things into his hands, and that he was come from God, and went to God; He riseth from supper, and laid aside his garments; and took a towel, and girded himself. After that he poureth water into a bason, and began to wash the disciples' feet, and to wipe them with the towel wherewith he was girded.*—JOHN 13:3–5

Knowing that He would soon be leaving His disciples, Jesus Christ knelt down, washed their feet, and showed His followers what it meant to be a true servant of God. What a selfless and humble task!

When you think of developing the mind of Christ, can you identify with His decision to be a servant? Are you willing to be involved in serving, witnessing, caring, and helping others? Are you willing to say, "Here am I, Lord; use me"? Are you willing to be expended for His cause and share His concern for others?

I heard of a pastor who challenged the men of his church to be more involved in service. He noticed the ladies were doing the majority of the work, and while this was wonderful, he wanted more of his men to become leaders in the church. During one of his messages he said, "I'm afraid some of you are taking the words to the song 'Take My Life and Let It Be,' and changing them to 'Take My Wife, and Let Me Be'!"

How we need men of God who will give themselves in service! We need men who will take on the mind of Christ and be servant leaders in their homes and in their churches! If Jesus Christ, the Creator and Sustainer of the world, would wash the disciples' feet, may we follow His example and reach out to others through weekly ministry and personal sacrifice.

Jesus Christ made a decision that involved the three steps outlined in Philippians: He made himself of no reputation; He took the form of a servant, and He humbled Himself. This was the greatest act of condescension the world has ever seen. Jesus Christ left His position at the right hand of the Father to come dwell on earth with the lowliest of mankind.

Christ's decision was not without a cost. There was the cost of self-sacrifice—He gave up His own prestige and His own privileges to meet our needs. Friend, ministry that costs you nothing accomplishes nothing. The fact that you are a Christian means that someone had to leave a comfort zone to tell you about Jesus Christ. Our Saviour decided to make the ultimate sacrifice, and He calls us to make the same sacrifice if we are going to become more like Him. If you will have the mind of Christ, you will decide to serve.

His Passion

Once you understand the enormity of Christ's decision, you can then begin to comprehend His passion. Philippians 2:8 states that Jesus "...*became obedient unto death, even the death of the cross*." Jesus Christ's passion was that we, a fallen race, would be reconciled to God. For this cause, He became obedient to the will of His Father.

This is illustrated when Jesus prayed in the Garden of Gethsemane, "...*Father, if thou be willing, remove this cup from me: nevertheless not my will, but thine, be done*" (Luke 22:42). I can't fully comprehend what Jesus was facing as He prayed this prayer. It wasn't the physical pain alone that so burdened Him but the overwhelming separation from His Father and carrying the sins of the entire world in His body—every lie, wicked act, every murder that had ever been committed.

What area of the Christian life seems difficult for you to obey? Which attitude of Christ is difficult for you to practice in your own life? Forgiveness? Humility? Perhaps it would do you well to visit Gethsemane in your mind and hear the words of Jesus, "...*Not my will, but thine, be done.*" It all boils down to your decision: Will you yield to the will of the Heavenly Father?

I challenge you to practice Christ-like obedience in your life and to voluntarily yield those sins you struggle with. Because of Jesus Christ's love and passion for you, He made Himself obedient unto death. He voluntarily died on the Cross for your sins. He was so passionate about saving you that He gave His own life!

The Bible says in Colossians 1:20, "*And, having made peace through the blood of his cross, by him to reconcile all things unto himself; by him, I say, whether they be things in earth, or things in heaven.*" Jesus Christ's blood was shed on the Cross. This was not of the Adamic or human bloodlines, but it was the very blood of God shed on Calvary for our sins.

Many times people are willing to serve others if it doesn't cost them anything or if it is convenient. I heard about a missionary in Brazil who once saw a sign hanging above a jewelry stand in a market place. It said, "Cheap Crosses." As the missionary told the story, I realized that there is no such thing as a cheap cross. Every cross has a cost.

Jesus' cross wasn't cheap or easy, yet He displayed His love by dying for our sins. Romans 5:8–9 says, *"But God commendeth his love toward us, in that, while we were yet sinners, Christ died for us. Much more then, being now justified by his blood, we shall be saved from wrath through him."*

What are you passionate about? Everybody has a passion. For some men, it's football or basketball. For others, it's hunting or fishing. For some ladies, it's shopping. If we took a poll and asked your friends what you are passionate about, what would they say? Do you have the mind of Christ? Would the poll reveal that you are passionate about spiritual things? Are you passionate about reaching the lost, sharing Christ, and serving God? Are you passionate about His purposes for your life?

Friend, when you have the mind of Christ, you will share the passion of Christ. You will identify with His heartbeat. You will live your life for a higher calling and for eternal purposes. As you begin to think like Him, you will share a concern for what He cares about. His passion will become your passion.

Are you developing the mind of Christ? Are you willing to leave your comfort zone to serve Him? Are you willing to be a bold witness for Jesus? Are you willing to wash the feet of those in need today? Jesus says that if we will lose our self-ambition, He will honor us. If we will lose our desire for things, He will provide for us. If we will lose our desire to be in control, He will give us power to follow Him. If we will lose our life, He will give us His very own.

My friend, there is no sacrifice too great for Jesus Christ. I have found when I sacrifice for Him, He has always blessed me beyond measure. As you are on this journey to become more like Jesus Christ, I challenge you to *"Let this mind be in you, which was also in Christ Jesus*" (Philippians 2:5). Pray and ask the Lord to help you start thinking like Him!

CHAPTER THIRTEEN

Living the Life of Christ
John 15:1–5

S everal years ago, a pastor in Northern California called and asked me to come preach for his church's three-day revival meeting. He said, "We are going to set up a large tent and spread some sawdust on the ground. Our choir is going to sing gospel music. If you would bring some old-fashioned preaching, we would really appreciate having you with us."

As we talked on the phone, I said, "This sounds like a great opportunity, but I am not always able to travel. Let me pray about this for a few days, and I will get back to you soon." Before we ended the conversation, the pastor told me that the other guest preacher was Dr. Lee Roberson from Chattanooga, Tennessee. My immediate response was "Brother, I have prayed about it, and I believe God would want me to come!"

Dr. Roberson has been a tremendous encouragement in my life. He pastored the same church for over forty-four years, and in his Christian life and ministry, he has seen thousands of people saved and baptized. He is a tremendous man of God, and I looked forward to the informal setting of the revival meeting when I would have an opportunity to spend some personal time with him.

On the first night of the meeting, Dr. Roberson and I drove over to the tent together. I had determined previously that I would wait until the second or third night to ask him the many questions I had written down in my planner. On that drive though, I became so excited that within sixty seconds of being in the car, I said, "Dr. Roberson, I need to ask you a question. I would like for you to share with me the key to obtaining God's blessings on my ministry."

I guess in my mind, I was looking for a simple solution—a specific formula. I will never forget Dr. Roberson's response that evening: "Brother Chappell, I want to encourage you with these thoughts. You must learn to die to self; that means dying to criticisms and to compliments. Second, as you die to self, you must seek to be filled with the Holy Spirit of God. This is the key to living the Christian life."

Since that meeting, I have found that when I am successful at applying those truths to my life, I experience great spiritual victory. When I am not dead to selfish desires or when I am quenching the Holy Spirit, God does not get the victory in my personal life or in my ministry. I believe many people want to mortify their flesh and yield their lives to the Holy Spirit of God, yet it is the everyday application of these truths that is a struggle for many people. The question then must be, "How can I live the life of Christ? How can I truly live the spiritual life of Christ without the interference of the flesh?" In this chapter, we are going to look at practical ways to live out the life of Christ.

The Life of Christ Is a Relationship To Enjoy

Before you read any further, I want you to clearly understand that the most important aspect of the Christian life is not rules or regulations; it is a relationship with Jesus Christ. Let's focus for a few moments on this word *relationship*—living out the life of Christ and allowing Him to live His life through us.

John 15:1–2 best illustrates our relationship with Christ by using a comparison between a vine and its branches, *"I am the true vine, and my Father is the husbandman. Every branch in me that beareth not fruit he taketh away: and every branch that beareth fruit, he purgeth it, that it may bring forth more fruit."*

In verse one, Jesus refers to Himself as *"the true vine."* In the Greek language, the word *true* is *alethinus*, which means "genuine." There are many vines—many different types of gods and religions—but there is only one true Vine—Jesus Christ.

Verses 4 and 5 say, *"Abide in me, and I in you. As the branch cannot bear fruit of itself, except it abide in the vine; no more can ye, except ye abide in me. I am the vine, ye are the branches: He that abideth in me, and I in him, the same bringeth forth much fruit: for without me ye can do nothing."* In verse 5, Jesus refers to His followers as the branches—extensions of Himself.

John 15:4 says, *"Abide in me, and I in you...."* As a Christian, you cannot live out the life of Christ unless you abide in Him. The Apostle Paul stated in Galatians 2:20 this reality as a testimony to his own life: *"I am crucified with Christ: nevertheless I live; yet not I, but Christ liveth in me: and the life which I now live in the flesh I live by the faith of the Son of God, who loved me, and gave himself for me."* In other words, Paul was saying, "The life I am living right now is not my own; it is Christ living through me."

We must recognize that Christ is the Vine; we are the branches; and He wants to live His life through us. He wants us to be representatives of Him in this lost and dying world. First John 2:27 states it this way, *"But the anointing which ye have received of him abideth in you...."* God wants to anoint our lives, but this only comes through the relationship we have with His Son, Jesus Christ.

This word *abide* means "to remain with Christ"—to spend time communing with Him and meditating on His Word. Today, in our upwardly mobile society, Americans aren't very good at abiding. We are constantly on the move—from job to job, city to city, church to church, and the list goes on.

Sometimes, in the midst of all those transitions our relationship with God is lost. We forget about fellowshipping and communing with Him through everyday Bible study and prayer. Instead of abiding in a joyful relationship with Christ, we live for selfish pleasures, quenching the work of the Holy Spirit in our lives.

Some people are so busy that they just can't seem to squeeze God into their day. But, the busier you are, the more you need God! Only He can give you the strength you need to live the life of Christ. Take time each day to meet with Him and to abide in Him. Christian, if you have not yet met with God today, take time right now to talk to Him. He's waiting to talk with you!

The Life of Christ Involves Obedience from the Heart

Once we understand that living the Christian life is primarily abiding in our relationship with Christ, we must then understand that this relationship involves obedience from the heart. Someone once said, "While the Christian life is primarily a relationship, it is clear to us that every relationship will produce its own rules. Every relationship generates laws consistent to the one to whom we are relating."

People will often criticize Christians who attend old-fashioned, Bible-believing Baptist churches. They'll say, "The problem with fundamental Christianity is that it's so legalistic. It's all about rules." I say, "Time out! The Christian life is not all about rules; it is about a relationship with Jesus Christ."

Yet, every worthwhile relationship will have its own set of rules that guide the relationship. Some people say, "I don't believe in that. I'm not going to any church that has rules. I'm about freedom!" Is that how you operate your marriage? Does your marriage matter, and do you think enough of that relationship to set up some principles by which you abide? Without principles, "Mr. Freedom" becomes "Mr. Divorced," because while this man is all about freedom, his reckless, lawless way of maintaining his marriage won't last. This may seem extreme, but what I am trying to illustrate is that every valuable relationship is governed by guidelines and rules.

Jesus said in Luke 6:46, *"And why call ye me, Lord, Lord, and do not the things which I say?"* We can have a relationship with Him, but it means nothing if we do not obey Him. A true relationship with Christ will produce obedience from a heart of love.

John 15:10 says, *"If ye keep my commandments, ye shall abide in my love; even as I have kept my Father's commandments, and abide in his love."* This verse tells us that we are to obey our Heavenly Father. Let's put aside the name Baptist or any other denomination. If you want to be a good Christian, then you must learn to obey God's commands. This is exactly what Jesus did in His life; He voluntarily submitted to the rules and the will of His Father.

My friend, that is not shallow Christianity; that is not legalistic Christianity; it is Bible Christianity. James 1:22 states, *"But be ye doers of the word, and not hearers only, deceiving your own selves,"* and John 14:23 tells us, *"…If a man love me, he will keep my words: and my Father will love him, and we will come unto him, and make our abode with him."*

In America today, most Christians think they can have a relationship with God while living in an ungodly fashion. This is a cheap substitute for true Christianity. True Christianity recognizes that God gave His all for us, and because we love Him, we will also give our all by obeying Him from a sincere heart.

The Life of Christ Is Guided by the Holy Spirit

You may say, "I am commanded to obey Jesus Christ, but that is so hard." I have good news for you! The Holy Spirit empowers you to understand and live the life of Christ. "Empowerment" is a buzzword in the corporate workplace, but in the Christian life, all true empowerment is from God! God will give us the resources we need, if we will only love Him enough to obey.

Ephesians 5:18 indicates that you are to live under the influence of the Holy Spirit: *"And be not drunk with wine, wherein is excess; but be filled with the Spirit."* When a person is intoxicated by liquor, he is under its influence—the liquor is controlling his actions. God wants you to be so filled with His Spirit, that you are under His power. When you are yielded to Him, you will desire to follow His commandments, and you will be able to carry them out, not by your own power but by the power that works within you.

The Holy Spirit reveals His power through the truth of God's Word. First Corinthians 2:9–10 says, *"But as it is written, Eye hath not seen, nor ear heard, neither have entered into the heart of man, the things which God hath prepared for them that love him. But God hath revealed them unto us by his Spirit: for the Spirit searcheth all things, yea, the deep things of God."*

We must avail ourselves to the Spirit's teaching through the Word of God. We need the Holy Spirit to empower us for the work of the Lord. When the Holy Spirit fills our lives, we will have no problem obeying Him, because He will generate both the desire and the strength to do the will of God.

Many distractions try to block and hinder our spiritual growth. For some men, it's football season. Erma Bombeck often said, "If a man watches three consecutive football games, he should be declared brain dead!" I am not condemning football or time spent in recreation. What I am trying to communicate is that God's truth will not be revealed to you, if you don't make time for it to happen, and if your relationship with God isn't your first priority.

You must be a person who studies the Bible, if God's Spirit is going to lead and guide you. John 14:26 states, *"But the Comforter, which is the Holy Ghost, whom the Father will send in my name, he shall teach you all things, and bring all things to your remembrance, whatsoever I have said unto you."* The great Illuminator of the spiritual life is not the pastor or the Sunday school teacher, but the Holy Spirit. We would do well to know Him and to listen to His still, small voice in our lives.

The Holy Spirit will both guide you and lead you away from sin. The Bible says in Galatians 5:16–18, *"This I say then, Walk in the Spirit, and ye shall not fulfil the lust of the flesh. For the flesh lusteth against the Spirit, and the Spirit against the flesh: and these are contrary the one to the other: so that ye cannot do the things that ye would. But if ye be led of the Spirit, ye are not under the law."*

We are not bound by the law; we are guided by the Spirit, which will lead us into the truth and show us the path of righteousness. As we obey the Holy Spirit and yield to the Word of God, He will show us true freedom.

Yes, the Holy Spirit was given to comfort us, but He was also given to guide us. Many people believe in a conscience that tells them right from wrong. It is the Holy Spirit that guides us and convicts our conscience from within. Never ignore the leading of the Holy Spirit within you. His leading is God's way of reminding you to follow Him!

Accept this wonderful gift from God. Ask Him to fill you with His Holy Spirit and to guide you today. You'll be amazed how He will intervene in your life and guide you moment by moment. As He does, obey His leading. Trust Him, and follow His Holy Spirit.

The Life of Christ Requires Endurance by His Grace

Living the life of Christ begins with a relationship. It is a relationship of abiding and walking with Him. That personal walk will produce a willing heart of obedience, as the Holy Spirit guides us day by day, and living the life of Christ requires endurance by His grace.

There are times I have wondered what it would be like to lay on the couch on Sunday mornings instead of going to church. There are days when I don't want to go out soulwinning. Enduring isn't easy, but we can *determine* to be faithful to God until we take our last breath here on earth. How can we endure? We must rely on God's grace for every situation in our lives.

Trials will come into your life. Every Christian faces temptation, opportunities to quit, times of weariness, and discouragement. Yet, living the life of Christ requires endurance. The Bible also calls this "patient continuance" in Romans 2:7. The Apostle Paul talked about finishing his course, running his race, and pressing toward the mark. Throughout Scripture, we are commanded to pursue the life of Christ with patience and endurance.

I heard about a lady who was so excited about the new sweater she was wearing. Her son said, "Mom, that's a nice sweater. You look just like the wheel of fortune." The mother replied, "Thank you, sweetheart, but I think you mean I look like Vanna White." "No," the son replied, "I mean the wheel." Sometimes life goes that way. When circumstances occur that are not exactly ego builders, it is easy to feel deflated and discouraged. Second Corinthians 9:8 says, *"And God is able to make all grace abound toward you; that ye, always having all sufficiency in all things, may abound to every good work."*

It is important to understand that God gives grace to the humble—to those who desire to possess the mind of Christ.

Remember it was Jesus' humility that enabled Him to leave the glory of Heaven to die on the Cross for your sins. Sometimes, the purpose for your trials is to bring you to a point of humility, so that God can give you the grace you need to endure your trials.

Look at 1 Peter 5:5, "...*for God resisteth the proud, and giveth grace to the humble*." God cannot give His grace to a heart that is filled with pride, so He must empty the heart of all pride through trying situations. Although these situations may deflate you, if you are seeking to live the life of Christ, you will be inflated by the Holy Spirit of God—strengthened by His power to endure and to continue in His grace.

A little boy insisted on giving his offering to the pastor after church one Sunday. The pastor kept telling him to give his money to the ushers. Finally, the little boy said in exasperation, "I really want to give my money to you. My dad says that you are the poorest preacher he has ever heard!" At times, we can be easily hurt, but when we come to God and admit our weaknesses and our failures, He always gives us enough grace to sustain us.

Psalm 51:17 reminds me that God is drawn to a repentant and submissive spirit: "*The sacrifices of God are a broken spirit: a broken and a contrite heart, O God, thou wilt not despise*." One man said, "Biblical obedience is not just compliance to some abstract law or rule. It is the submissive response to the Person of the Holy Spirit who has revealed the will of God to us through His Word."

Christ-likeness is not following an ethical ideal; it is the manifestation of God's Spirit in the life of a believer. We can enjoy a personal relationship with God Himself! When we experience this relationship, we will obey Him from a heart of love through the power of the Holy Spirit. Even though this wonderful new life will contain struggles, God provides His grace for those who humbly ask for it, and He will give us the strength day by day to finish our course with joy.

CHAPTER FOURTEEN

Expressing the Life of Christ
Ephesians 4:17–27

Athletes from across our country and around the world are constantly preparing for the most prestigious competitive event in world history—the Olympic Games. Every four years, thousands of hopeful young people are holding on to the dream of winning a gold medal. These athletes know that if their dream is to become a reality, they must put off old habits—a poor diet, unsuitable apparel, and low-impact workouts. If they are to be competitive in their field, they must acquire those necessary skills and disciplines that will enable success and victory.

In this race called the Christian life, God says we must put on Jesus Christ if we are to be winners. We must be an expression of Him if we are going to experience true success. It is God's plan that our lives would be vibrant expressions of the life of Christ from within—that we would truly reflect the nature and character of Jesus Christ in our daily lives.

This expression of the life of Christ must be generated from within by the power of the Holy Spirit, but it should also be clearly seen in our outward lifestyle. Just as an Olympic athlete makes daily choices in behavior and diet that furthers the dream of the heart, a faithful Christian will make lifestyle changes from a heart desire to reflect Jesus Christ more accurately.

What does this expression of the life of Christ look like in the life of a Christian?

We Must Walk a Different Walk

This I say therefore, and testify in the Lord, that ye henceforth walk not as other Gentiles walk, in the vanity of their mind.—EPHESIANS 4:17

God intends for the behavior of a believer to be radically different from the behavior of an unbeliever. Many Christians are being told that it does not matter how they live, and churches are helping them feel comfortable in sinful lifestyles. The fact is that God is calling believers to be distinctly different. Grace and Christian liberty do not give us a license to live in sin; they give us the freedom to walk in the light and to be transformed by God's power. Romans 12:2 says, *"And be not conformed to this world: but be ye transformed...."*

In Ephesians 4:17–18, Paul describes the sinful condition of the unsaved world, they *"...walk, in the vanity of their mind, Having the understanding darkened, being alienated from the life of God through the ignorance that is in them, because of the blindness of their heart."*

Verse 17 speaks about *"the vanity of their mind."* Vanity means "empty." In our world today, empty philosophies abound, and they are a reflection of the world's darkened spiritual condition. The Bible speaks of them in Colossians 2:8–9, *"Beware lest any man spoil you through philosophy and vain deceit, after the tradition of men, after the rudiments of the world, and not after Christ. For in him dwelleth all the fulness of the Godhead bodily.*" God says that we must stand guard over our hearts and minds, so we are not led astray and deceived by the empty, vain philosophies of the world.

Paul describes the world's sinful condition as "darkened understanding." In other words, those without Christ are spiritually blind—their understanding is darkened concerning the things of God. The Bible tells us in 2 Corinthians 4:4, "*In whom the god of this world hath blinded the minds of them which believe not, lest the light of the glorious gospel of Christ, who is the image of God, should shine unto them.*" Satan has blinded unsaved people from seeing the truth of God, which makes them vulnerable to the false teaching and vain philosophies that abound today.

For instance, some men believe in reincarnation—that after death, they will return to this world in animal form or in some higher state of consciousness. Others believe they are intrinsically good, and according to their humanistic philosophies, they don't need a Saviour. Still others believe they are becoming a god themselves, without the help of God and the truth of the Gospel. Many ideologies are prevalent in the world today, but the Bible speaks of them as being vain imaginations and darkened philosophies. These false teachings are the product of hearts and minds that are alienated from God.

Paul continues his description of the world's darkened condition in Ephesians 4:18, "*…being alienated from the life of God through the ignorance that is in them, because of the blindness of their heart.*" Without the illumination of God's Holy Spirit, men's hearts are blind, and they are alienated from an understanding of God. Even the wisest philosophers of this world, such as Socrates or Nietzsche are spiritually empty without the truth.

Our lives should contrast the sinful, depraved nature of lost men. Verse 19 describes the depravity of mankind, "*Who being past feeling have given themselves over unto lasciviousness* (wicked living), *to work all uncleanness with greediness."* Notice the phrase *"past feeling."* This speaks of the numbness of soul that is experienced by a God-rejecting person. There are some people who have become so involved in wickedness—so darkened to the truth—that they experience spiritual numbness. It is as if Novocain has been injected into their hearts.

For example, have you ever thought of how vital pain is in our physical lives? No one enjoys pain, but pain alerts us to a problem. Pain is a gift that warns us and calls for a response. Furthermore, a doctor must be able to identify the pain before he can give a proper diagnosis, and if a sick person does not or cannot sense pain, it is considered a very serious factor.

Even so, it is a spiritually dangerous thing when you stop feeling the pricking conviction of God in your heart. Christians who embrace the wicked philosophies of this world can quickly lose their sense of what is right and wrong. We can lose our ability to feel the conviction of God. It is a spiritually dangerous thing when a Christian can engage in demonic or lustful activities with no rebuke of the conscience. In this case, the conscience is seared and the heart is past sensing God's work within it.

The Bible speaks of this in Mark 7:22–23, *"Thefts, covetousness, wickedness, deceit, lasciviousness, an evil eye, blasphemy, pride, foolishness: All these evil things come from within, and defile the man."* When someone gives himself over to wickedness, his life is defiled. His conscience is seared with a hot iron, and he no longer understands the truth. Ephesians 4:19 says, *"Who being past feeling have given themselves over unto lasciviousness, to work all uncleanness with greediness."* Notice the word *work.* It means, "to take pains to do your best." Because of their dark, depraved spiritual nature, there are people in the world who literally go to great effort to live defiled, unclean lives. Many people work harder at living in sin than a sincere, God-dependent Christian would work at living for Christ! Many people exercise themselves in ungodliness. Paul was telling the Christians at Ephesus that they must live different lives—they must walk a different walk if they are to express the life of Christ.

We Must Be Different to Make a Difference

As Christians, we are not here to tread water or to "barely hold on" until Jesus comes. We are here to make a difference! God has called us to be different and to make a difference. This truth is clearly shown in the Word of God.

> *That ye put off concerning the former conversation the old man, which is corrupt according to the deceitful lusts; And be renewed in the spirit of your mind; And that ye put on the new man, which after God is created in righteousness and true holiness.*—Ephesians 4:22–24

Once we have received Christ, the Holy Spirit creates a new disposition within us—a disposition very different from that of lost men. Colossians 3:9–10 states, "*Lie not one to another, seeing that ye have put off the old man with his deeds; And have put on the new man, which is renewed in knowledge after the image of him that created him.*" God commands us to put off our old man and old deeds and to put on the new man in Christ.

The above passage in Ephesians tells us that the old desires are "*corrupt according to the deceitful lusts.*" The new nature of the Holy Spirit will create holiness, love, and godliness, but the old man will only produce corruption. The Bible says, "*For the wages of sin is death….*" (Romans 6:23). When we sow seeds of corruption, we will reap a life of spiritual death. We are called to express Christ's life and to live differently to the glory of God. This difference begins with the way we think! Ephesians 4:23 teaches us, "*And be renewed in the spirit of your mind.*" The entire direction of your life can be traced to the way you think. The

Bible says, *"For as he thinketh in his heart, so is he..."* (Proverbs 23:7), and *"...out of the abundance of the heart the mouth speaketh"* (Matthew 12:34).

In contrast to the darkened, blinded minds of the world, God wants to renew and transform our minds by His power. God's Word is the tool the Holy Spirit will use to give you a new way of thinking and living. Philippians 4:8 illustrates this truth: *"Finally, brethren, whatsoever things are true, whatsoever things are honest, whatsoever things are just, whatsoever things are pure, whatsoever things are lovely, whatsoever things are of good report; if there be any virtue, and if there be any praise, think on these things."* A different life begins with a different mind, which begins with meditating upon the Word of God on a daily basis.

It is important that you put off the old man, but to really make a difference, you must put on the new nature of Christ. *"And that ye put on the new man, which after God is created in righteousness and true holiness"* (Ephesians 4:24). The old man is the inherited sin nature, but the new man is the nature of Christ placed into us by the presence of His Holy Spirit. Romans 5:12 says, *"Wherefore, as by one man sin entered into the world, and death by sin; and so death passed upon all men, for that all have sinned."* Adam, the spiritual head of the human race, chose to sin, and his sin was then passed to all men. That is why every one of us needs to be born again into the Spirit of Christ—every one of us needs a new nature.

As Christians, we will still battle between the flesh and the spirit every day. It is a daily reality that the flesh wars against the spirit—our new nature in Christ.

As believers, we are commanded to make a daily choice to live differently than our flesh would dictate. We're not to be operated or led by our flesh but rather by the Spirit of God. God has given us the power of His Holy Spirit and a new nature that is capable of doing right. We must daily choose to put on that new nature and to walk in newness of life. That new life will be the life of Christ and will be distinctly different from those who do not know Him.

For instance, someone who is putting on the new man will speak differently from the world. The Bible says, "...*Out of the abundance of the heart the mouth speaketh*" (Matthew 12:34). Ephesians 4:25 says, "*Wherefore putting away lying, speak every man truth with his neighbour: for we are members one of another.*"

The Holy Spirit is the Spirit of Truth. John 15:26 says, "*But when the Comforter is come, whom I will send unto you from the Father, even the Spirit of truth, which proceedeth from the Father, he shall testify of me.*" When you are yielding to God's Spirit, there will be a transformation in your speech. Your words will be true and will be seasoned with the grace of God.

Someone who is putting on the new man will handle anger differently. Ephesians 4:26 tells us, "*Be ye angry, and sin not: let not the sun go down upon your wrath.*" Isn't this an interesting thought—be angry, and sin not? You may say, "I thought anger was a sin. What is this verse saying?" Did you know that it is okay to be angry for a righteous cause? You can be angry at a problem, but you cannot be angry toward a person. For example, you should be angry at liquor if it has turned your husband into an alcoholic, but you should not be angry at your husband. You should be angry and hate the sin of abortion, but you should not hate the abortionist.

There is nothing wrong with being angry for a righteous cause, but a Christian who is angry toward people is not reflecting the life of Christ. The Bible says in Ephesians 4:27 that anger gives place to the devil. Therefore, we must put off the temperament of the old man, and claim a new disposition that reflects Christ. We must yield to God's presence within and allow His life to be clearly seen through us.

Are you willing to be different? As a Christian, you are to be different by design. God has called you to stand out from the crowd. Don't hide your light. Don't be ashamed of Christ. Be willing to be different and trust by faith that He will use you to make a difference!

We Must Love Christ if We Will Be Different

God is concerned that our motives for change be right. Throughout Scripture, He commands us to love Him and live for Him with all of our hearts. He wants all external changes to flow from an internal love and commitment to Him. Unfeigned love for Christ is the great motivator and the key to genuinely expressing His life. You may attempt to fake the Christian life for a time, but only a heart love will compel you to walk with Him faithfully. Only a sincere heart will allow His transforming power to create true spiritual renewal.

Ephesians 4:19–21 says, "*Who being past feeling have given themselves over unto lasciviousness, to work all uncleanness with greediness. But ye have not so learned Christ; If so be that ye have heard him, and have been taught by him, as the truth is in Jesus.*" These verses tell us that we did not learn wickedness and ungodliness from Jesus Christ, because He is the One who teaches us the truth. Therefore, we must have a relationship with Him if we are going to put off the old man and put on the new nature. It is not so much a matter of discipline, as it is devotion. How much do you know and love Jesus Christ? When you truly know Him, you will live a life that brings glory and honor to His name, and that life will be genuinely motivated and generated from a sincere heart.

The Apostle Paul was not pointing the Ephesian Christians to a creed or a list of commandments, he was pointing them to a person. He wasn't pointing them to rules, he was pointing them to a relationship. He said, *"But ye have not so learned Christ"* (vs. 20). Christianity is not a system of religion, but rather a relationship with the person of Jesus Christ.

Just as a marital relationship begins at the wedding altar, a relationship with Jesus Christ begins at salvation. Once we accept Him, our relationship and love should continue to grow and develop. Deuteronomy 6:5 says, *"And thou shalt love the LORD thy God with all thine heart, and with all thy soul, and with all thy might."* First, we meet the Lord, and then, we come to love Him. With that love comes the desire to put on the new man—to live and express His love in a dark world.

There is no greater motivation and change agent in the Christian life than the love of Christ. A right relationship with Christ will give you victory over the mental and spiritual darkness of this world. It will clarify your thoughts, enlighten your understanding, quicken your conscience, and strengthen your resolve to live a life separated unto Him. The closer you draw to Him, the further you will be from the world. The more different you are from the world, the greater the difference you can make for Christ.

> *And the Word was made flesh, and dwelt among us,*
> *(and we beheld his glory, the glory as of the only begotten*
> *of the Father,) full of grace and truth.*—JOHN 1:14

False religions corrupt, and churches get sidetracked. But Jesus Christ is the same yesterday, today, and forever. Ephesians 4:21 says, *"...the truth is in Jesus."* The way of the world ends in defilement, decay, and death; but the way of the Christian is new and abundant life in Christ.

During World War II, a pastor in England would see businesses in his city that had been ravaged by bombs. Often, the owners would clear away the rubbish, and place a sign outside that said, "Business As Usual." Many Christians are doing their "business as usual." They are going about their lives without allowing God to change and renew them spiritually. They have trusted Christ, but they are not going on unto perfection. They are not maturing in Christ and expressing His life to a lost world. God desires to transform your life. Then, through that transformation, He desires to express the life of Christ through you to a dark world. Don't allow your life to be "business as usual"—start advertising that your life is "under new management." Let Christ express His life through you today.

CHAPTER FIFTEEN

Sharing the Message of Christ
John 4:1–30

One of the foundational reasons for becoming like Christ is that we may share His message effectively with a lost and dying world. God is looking for people who are conforming to His image and who are growing in His grace—not perfect, but growing more like Him—to share the Gospel message with the lost.

> *Who hath saved us, and called us with an holy calling, not according to our works, but according to his own purpose and grace, which was given us in Christ Jesus before the world began.*—2 TIMOTHY 1:9

A young salesman was disappointed about losing a big sale, and as he talked with his sales manager, he lamented, "I guess it just proves you can lead a horse to water, but you can't make him drink." The manager replied, "Son, take my advice: your job is not to make him drink. Your job is to make him thirsty." As Christians, our job is to expose the thirst for the living water of Christ that already exists in a lost heart. Our lives should be so filled with Christ that we literally create a thirst for the love of God in the lives of unbelievers.

Many years ago in St. Louis, a lawyer visited a Christian to transact some business. Before the two men parted, the client said, "I've often wanted to ask you a question, but I have been afraid to do so." "What do you want to know?" asked the lawyer. The man replied, "I've wondered why you're not a Christian." The man hung his head, "I know enough about the Bible to realize that it says no drunkard can enter the kingdom of God, and you know my weakness!" "You're avoiding my question," continued the believer. "Well, truthfully, I can't recall anyone ever explaining how to become a Christian." Picking up a Bible, the client read some passages showing that all are under condemnation, but that Christ came to save the lost by dying on the Cross for their sins. "By receiving Him as your substitute and Redeemer," he said, "You can be forgiven. If you're willing to receive Jesus, let's pray together." The lawyer agreed, and when it was his turn he exclaimed, "Oh, Jesus, I am a slave to drink. One of your servants has shown me how to be saved. Oh, God, forgive my sins and help me overcome the power of this terrible habit in my life." The lawyer was converted right at that moment. His name was C. I. Scofield, who later edited the reference Bible that bears his name.

Although there is much relativism and spiritual confusion in our world today, the message of Christ has not changed since the first century. The Apostle Paul distinctly mentions the Gospel in 1 Corinthians 15:1–4: *"Moreover, brethren, I declare unto you the gospel which I preached unto you, which also ye have received, and wherein ye stand; By which also ye are saved, if ye keep in memory what I preached unto you, unless ye have believed in vain. For I delivered unto you first of all that which I also received, how that Christ died for our sins according to the scriptures; And that he was buried, and that he rose again the third day according to the scriptures.*" Jesus had a purpose in coming to this earth—to die for our sins and then be raised up again for our justification. As we conform our lives into His image, He asks us to join Him in fulfilling His purpose by sharing the message of the Gospel. Jesus spoke these words to His disciples in John 20:21, *"Then said Jesus to them again, Peace be unto you: as my Father hath sent me, even so send I you."*

As we are becoming more like Christ it only seems natural, or may I say spiritual, that we would share His message regularly to help others know Jesus as their personal Saviour.

Christ's Purpose in Coming to the Earth

For the Son of man is come to seek and to save that which was lost.—LUKE 19:10

Jesus Christ came to seek out and to bring salvation to those who were lost and without Him. I always enjoy reading how the Lord personally gave the Gospel to others. John 4:1–5 gives an account of how the Lord shared eternal truth with a woman in great need: *"When therefore the Lord knew how the Pharisees had heard that Jesus made and baptized more disciples than John, (Though Jesus himself baptized not, but his disciples,) He left Judaea, and departed again into Galilee. And he must needs go through Samaria. Then cometh he to a city of Samaria, which is called Sychar, near to the parcel of ground that Jacob gave to his son Joseph."*

Christ's purpose in coming to earth took Him a necessary way. Verse 4 says, *"He must needs go through Samaria."* In others words, He felt compelled to go this particular route. Jesus Christ was following the leadership of His Heavenly Father, and He was filled with the Holy Spirit.

Psalm 37:23 says, *"The steps of a good man are ordered by the LORD: and he delighteth in his way."* If a good man's steps are ordered by the Lord, how much more were the steps of Jesus Christ! His purpose of reaching lost people took Him to a necessary place where there was spiritual need.

Have you ever felt moved by the Spirit of God to go a particular direction and speak to someone about Jesus Christ? Have you ever felt that inner compulsion to tell someone else— maybe a co-worker, friend, or relative—about salvation? That is what Jesus experienced on this particular day.

Jesus left the area where His disciples were baptizing. He was also possibly leaving a schism that was developing with the Pharisees because of His popularity. John 4:1–3 states, *"When therefore the Lord knew how the Pharisees had heard that Jesus made and baptized more disciples than John, (Though Jesus himself baptized not, but his disciples,) He left Judaea, and departed again into Galilee."* He went to the well of Sychar, to a divine appointment arranged by His Heavenly Father.

When you are living your life according to the purpose of Christ, there is no such thing as an accident. He wants us to be witnesses of Him throughout the normal, everyday circumstances of our lives and He will often lead us into divine appointments to represent Him to others.

On this day, Jesus' divine appointment took Him to a needy woman. The Bible says in John 4:7–10, *"There cometh a woman of Samaria to draw water: Jesus saith unto her, Give me to drink. (For his disciples were gone away unto the city to buy meat.) Then saith the woman of Samaria unto him, How is it that thou, being a Jew, askest drink of me, which am a woman of Samaria? for the Jews have no dealings with the Samaritans. Jesus answered and said unto her, If thou knewest the gift of God, and who it is that saith to thee, Give me to drink; thou wouldest have asked of him, and he would have given thee living water."* The Bible is clear that this woman had not put her faith in Jesus Christ, and she had experienced terrible marital and extramarital difficulties. She did not live a life of high moral standards. More than likely, she was the subject of gossip and ridicule, yet Jesus says in John 4:7, *"…Give me to drink."*

Imagine this scene. The Creator of the universe is asking this needy woman for a drink of water. Why? So that He could offer her something even greater—living water. Jesus came to offer the forgiveness of sin. He came to quench the thirst of a lost world. Matthew 9:12 says, *"But when Jesus heard that, he said unto them, They that be whole need not a physician, but they that are sick."*

His Promise for Those Who Receive His Gift

Jesus answered and said unto her, If thou knewest the gift of God, and who it is that saith to thee, Give me to drink; thou wouldest have asked of him, and he would have given thee living water.—JOHN 4:10

God has given a special promise to those who receive His gift. The Scriptures call this gift living water and an eternal well of water springing up in those who believe. Romans 6:23 also mentions this gift, *"For the wages of sin is death; but the gift of God is eternal life through Jesus Christ our Lord."* Salvation is paid in full by Jesus Christ and is offered to each of us as a free gift. Ephesians 2:8 says, *"For by grace are ye saved through faith; and that not of yourselves: it is the gift of God."* If we have to do anything for eternal life, it is not a gift.

My wife and I have four wonderful children who are all gifted with different talents and abilities. I learned many years ago, that the best back-scratcher in our family is my daughter, Kristine. Every once in a while, I will call Kristine over to my chair and say, "See this dollar right here? You can have it if you will scratch my back for a minute." Many times she will gladly take the dollar, and then she will tell me that she will be back to scratch my back later.

The moment I tell my daughter, "You can have a dollar *if...*" the back-scratch ceases to be a gift. My friend, if we have to follow sacraments, baptism, or do anything to obtain salvation, it is not a gift. When it comes to salvation, let's not muddy the waters with religious tradition. Let's come back to the Bible!

God's gift is not reserved for a select few; it is freely given to a world that is living in sinful conditions. Romans 1:16 says, "*For I am not ashamed of the gospel of Christ: for it is the power of God unto salvation to every one that believeth; to the Jew first, and also to the Greek.*" Likewise, John 4 gives an account of the indignation that was taking place during the time of Jesus Christ. In verse 9, as Jesus talked with the Samaritan woman, she said, "*...How is it that thou, being a Jew, askest drink of me, which am a woman of Samaria? for the Jews have no dealings with the Samaritans.*"

Racial tension was high between the Samaritans and the Jews, and most Jews would have never stopped to talk to this woman. The fact that Jesus did, shows us His amazing and impartial love for all men. His gift of salvation is available freely to all men!

Romans 1:17–18 speaks of the iniquity that is so prevalent in the world: "*For therein is the righteousness of God revealed from faith to faith: as it is written, The just shall live by faith. For the wrath of God is revealed from heaven against all ungodliness and unrighteousness of men, who hold the truth in unrighteousness.*"

Fornication and adultery were the essence of the Samaritan woman's life. In John 4:16–18, Jesus exchanged these words with her: "*Jesus saith unto her, Go, call thy husband, and come hither. The woman answered and said, I have no husband. Jesus said unto her, Thou hast well said, I have no husband: For thou hast had five husbands; and he whom thou now hast is not thy husband: in that saidst thou truly.*"

As long as this woman attempted to hide behind a cloak of religion or righteousness, she could not be saved. Jesus met her where she was, as a sinner, but He could not help her until she admitted her need for salvation. Jesus brought her face to face with this fact in John 4:14–15, *"But whosoever drinketh of the water that I shall give him shall never thirst; but the water that I shall give him, shall be in him a well of water springing up into everlasting life. The woman saith unto him, Sir, give me this water, that I thirst not, neither come hither to draw."*

My wife and I were out soulwinning one day and we visited a family that had attended our church. The husband desired to serve the Lord, but his wife was not a Christian—she had never placed her faith in Christ. As we sat on the couch in their living room, we made small talk for a while. Then I asked the wife this question: "If you were to die today, where would you spend eternity?" As she lit a cigarette, she said, "I don't think anyone can know the answer to that question."

She began to argue and talk roughly about her past and the hypocrisy she had seen amongst Christians. I soon realized that sitting before me was a woman who had been deeply wounded. After she mentioned her recent abortion, she began to weep. "They told me it wouldn't matter," she said.

She told me about some other experiences in her life—the parties, the drugs, and the immorality. Finally I said, "You don't need to tell us this. No matter where you have been or what you have done, we are here to tell you that Jesus still loves you. He wants to forgive your sin." She looked at us in disbelief as she continued smoking and talking.

She did not accept Christ as her Saviour, and my wife and I left that visit feeling as if maybe we had not said all the right words. We began to pray for her. Two weeks later during our church's invitation, this dear lady walked down the aisle, and my wife had the privilege of leading her to Christ.

Sometimes the devil will make people who have lived in immorality or wickedness feel like there is no hope—that there is no way Jesus would want them. I am glad that Jesus Christ died for everyone—black or white, rich or poor, good or bad. Jesus offers forgiveness to all people, not to a select few.

After the Samaritan woman was faced with the fact that she needed living water, she began to argue with Jesus in John 4:20: *"Our fathers worshipped in this mountain; and ye say, that in Jerusalem is the place where men ought to worship."* This woman had no understanding of the truth. Her people were living in idolatry. They had built a rival temple at Gerazim because the Jews had rejected them during the days of Ezra. This woman was basically saying, "I have a church. I have a denomination and a belief system. What's wrong with that?" She knew a few religious arguments, but she did not know the Saviour.

His Power To Provide Salvation

Jesus not only came with a promise, He came with the power to back up His promise. His power is seen in His attributes. John 4:23–24 says, *"But the hour cometh, and now is, when the true worshippers shall worship the Father in spirit and in truth: for the Father seeketh such to worship him. God is a Spirit: and they that worship him must worship him in spirit and in truth."*

Salvation is something only God can provide. In verse 23, Jesus foretells the time when the place of worship won't be so important, because the Person of worship will have preeminence. That is why He says in verse 24 that mankind will be able to worship Him in Spirit and in truth.

A similar passage says, *"And I will pray the Father, and he shall give you another Comforter, that he may abide with you for ever; Even the Spirit of truth; whom the world cannot receive, because it seeth him not, neither knoweth him: but ye know him; for he dwelleth with you, and shall be in you"* (John 14:16–17). Once Christ saves us, the Holy Spirit comes and dwells in our hearts. He is the One who gives us the power to share the message of Christ boldly.

Christ's power is also seen in John 4:25–26, *"The woman saith unto him, I know that Messias cometh, which is called Christ: when he is come, he will tell us all things. Jesus saith unto her, I that speak unto thee am he."* The words *Christ* and *Messiah* are synonyms. They mean "the anointed One." In verse 26, Jesus is accepting and claiming the term Messiah.

In these verses, Jesus not only promises salvation, but He claims He has the power to provide it. He has the power to change us and use us for His glory, as we shine as lights for Him in a lost world.

Dr. Paul Brand was speaking to a medical college in India on Matthew 5:16: *"Let your light so shine before men, that they may see your good works, and glorify your Father which is in heaven."* He had placed an oil lamp in front of the lectern, and a cotton wick was burning from the shallow dish of oil. As he preached, the lamp's oil ran out, the wick burned dry, and the smoke made him cough. He immediately used this opportunity to say, "Some of us here are like this wick. We are trying to shine for the glory of God, but we stink. That's what happens when we use ourselves as the fuel for our witness rather than the Holy Spirit. Wicks can last indefinitely–burning brightly and without irritating smoke—if the fuel, the Holy Spirit, is in constant supply."

The woman at the well came to realize that she was in the presence of the Messiah, and after her salvation, she immediately began to witness for Him: *"The woman then left her waterpot, and went her way into the city, and saith to the men, Come, see a man, which told me all things that ever I did: is not this the Christ?"* (John 4:28–29).

If you truly understood the promise of the Messiah, you would be more apt to leave your waterpots—those hobbies, occupations, and recreations that distract us from being a witness for Christ. The vast majority of people in your city do not attend a Bible-believing church. Most of them do not know Jesus Christ personally, and many have never heard of His love. Many of them are in situations like the woman at the well—they have tremendous spiritual needs in their hearts and lives.

Their need is why God placed you here—to share the message of Christ with the lost. What about you, Christian? Are you burning brightly as a witness for Christ? Remember that a true messenger of God will first seek to conform to His image. The change must take place in the messenger before the message will have a life-changing impact on the listeners. Are you allowing Christ's power and strength to shine brightly through your life? Does your presence create a thirst for God's love in others? When you experience Christ's presence and power, you won't be able to keep from sharing His great love with others—it will come naturally from your heart!

In your community right now there are men and women seeking life changes. Much like the Samaritan woman, people are crying out—looking for hope. You have the answer, but is your life a testimony to your knowledge of the truth? Go make someone thirsty by showing them the love of Christ, and then quench that thirst by sharing the truth of Christ!

CONCLUSION

T he Christian life is an amazing and wonderful journey of transformation that begins at salvation and ends when we meet the Lord. It is a marathon—a journey that requires patience, endurance, and steady transformation. If you haven't noticed, although God desires to conform you to the image of Christ, He doesn't seem to be in a hurry, since He's planning to take the rest of your natural life for the process to occur.

I believe one of the most frustrating experiences of the Christian life is when we become impatient with God and His work in us. If you are in love with the Lord Jesus, then you probably desire to be more like Him—right now! You probably don't want to wait. I have often wished the process were more immediate, too!

Perhaps this is why God says in Hebrews 10 that we must have patience. He says in Hebrews 10:35–37, *"Cast not away therefore your confidence, which hath great recompence of reward.*

For ye have need of patience, that, after ye have done the will of God, ye might receive the promise. For yet a little while, and he that shall come will come, and will not tarry."

Think about these words: *"Cast not away therefore your confidence."* God is telling us not to quit. He's telling us to endure until the end. He's saying that we can rest in confidence that He is continuing His work, whether or not we see it, sense it, or understand it.

Then He says, " *For ye have need of patience...."* I believe the key to abiding in Christ and becoming more like Him is simply patience. I encourage you, friend, as we draw these pages to a close, to have patience. Let patience have her perfect work, that you may be perfect or mature (James 1:4). Let God take the time He wants to shape you, mold you, and transform you into the image of His dear Son. Don't become frustrated in the process. Rest in His grace. Wait on Him. As a piece of clay, stay on the potter's wheel, and let Him gently conform you to Christ one day at a time.

He promises in this passage that your endurance *"hath great recompence of reward."* He says that the wait is worth it! You may not be as far along as you wish you were spiritually. Yet, if you've been saved for more than a few years, you can probably look back and see some amazing growth that has already taken place in your life.

Stand strong in the same confidence that has brought you this far. Continue abiding daily in the presence of Jesus Christ. Always keep your relationship with Him the priority of your life, and know that while you do, He is doing His supernatural work within you. There is never a moment that He is not transforming you, so long as you are abiding in Him. There is never a moment when you are not becoming more like Christ, so long as you are walking with Him. His Word is always effectual and His Holy Spirit is always changing you if you have a yielded heart.

What a wonderful journey these studies have been for me in the preparation. I have fallen in love with the Lord Jesus all over again, and I hope you have too! I pray that God has used these truths to compel you to enter His presence, to abide with Him daily, and to allow His Holy Spirit to gradually transform you to become more like Christ.

You have a Saviour who desires to give you abundant joy, amazing love, renewed strength, and much fruit. You have an eternal purpose in His plan, and you have His guiding presence every moment of every day. I pray that you will abide with Him and become more like Him—today, tomorrow, and for the rest of your life.

Additional Sunday School Resources

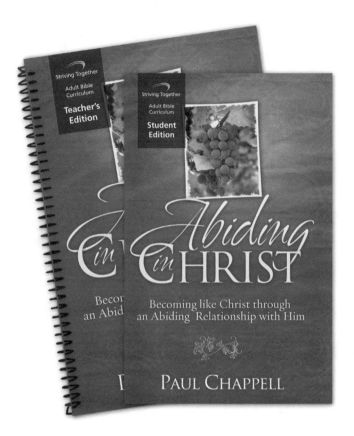

Use *Abiding in Christ* as an Adult Sunday School Curriculum!

The companion teacher's guide and student guide make this book a perfect curriculum for adult classes in your church.

For more information visit
strivingtogether.com

Also available from
strivingtogether publications

It's a Wonderful Life
In these pages, Terrie Chappell shares a practical, biblical approach to loving your family and serving Jesus Christ. Her humorous and down-to-earth insight will encourage your heart and equip you to love the life to which God has called you. (280 Pages, Hardback)

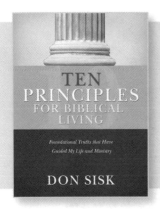

Ten Principles for Biblical Living
Drawing from over fifty-two years of ministry experience and a profound impact on worldwide missions, Dr. Don Sisk shares ten biblical and practical principles that have shaped his life and ministry. These principles will call you to a renewed life of service for Jesus Christ and are perfect for sharing with others as well. (120 Pages, Hardback)

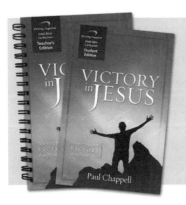

Victory in Jesus
Teacher's and Student's Edition
In these lessons, your students will discover God's purpose for suffering and His method for overcoming trials. They will learn how to face adversity in the light of God's Word and live a victorious and fulfilling Christian life!

Also available from
strivingtogether publications

done.

Specifically created to be placed into the hands of an unsaved person and a perfect gift for first-time church visitors, this new mini book explains the Gospel in crystal clear terms. The reader will journey step by step through biblical reasoning that concludes at the Cross and a moment of decision. This tool will empower your whole church family to share the Gospel with anyone! (100 Pages, Mini Paperback)

Your Pastor and You

Wise Christians find and establish strong relationships with godly pastors and choose to fight for those relationships. They encourage their pastor, accept his spiritual watchcare in their lives, and support him in his call to serve God. (48 Pages, Mini Paperback)

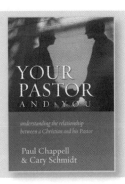

A Maze of Grace

If you or someone you love is enduring a season of suffering, this booklet will provide a cup of fresh water for the journey. Each chapter shares God's wisdom, encouragement, and insight. Each turn of the page will bring fresh hope and trust in the unseen hand of a loving God. (64 Pages, Mini Paperback)

Visit us online

strivingtogether.com

dailyintheword.org

wcbc.edu

lancasterbaptist.org